Understanding Scripture

What Is the Bible and How Does It Speak?

John F. Balchin

InterVarsity Press
Downers Grove
Illinois 60515

InterVarsity Press is the book-publishing division of Inter-Varsity Christian Fellowship, a student movement active on campus at hundreds of universities, colleges and schools of nursing. For information about local and regional activities, write IVCF, 233 Langdon St., Madison, WI 53703.

Distributed in Canada through InterVarsity Press, 1875 Leslie St., Unit 10, Don Mills, Ontario M3B 2M5, Canada.

Unless otherwise stated, quotations from the Bible are from the Revised Standard Version, copyrighted 1946, 1952, © 1971, 1973, by the Division of Christian Education, National Council of the Churches of Christ in the U.S.A. and used by permission.

ISBN 0-87784-875-0

Printed in the United States of America

Library of Congress Cataloging in Publication Data

Balchin, John F., 1937-
    Understanding Scripture.

    Includes bibliographical references.
    1. Bible–Criticism, interpretation, etc.
2. Bible–Hermeneutics.   I. Title.
BS511.2.B34   1981   220.6'1   81-8271
ISBN 0-87784-875-0   AACR2

15	14	13	12	11	10	9	8	7	6	5	4	3	2	1
93	92	91	90	89	88	87	86	85	84	83	82	81		

What's it all about?

'Why shouldn't I go down to the pub with my friends?' said Bill. 'After all, Paul said, "By all means save some." How can I witness to them if I don't have a drink with them?'

'But can't you see,' protested Jane, 'the Bible says, "Come out from them, and be separate from them"? You're just compromising the gospel by what you're doing.'

And so they hammered on for most of the evening. But who was right? After all, they both had a Bible verse to support their arguments.

Or what about Steve who was so eager to share his faith with Peter, only to be stonewalled with the objection, 'But you can't believe the Bible! Science has disproved it. What with all we know about evolution nowadays, you're not going to tell me that it all happened in six days!'

'But...' stammered Steve, although he didn't really have an answer to that one.

It was harder still for Pauline. She was really in love with John, but because they were both involved in demanding college courses, they wouldn't be able to get married for quite some time. Then one evening John told her that he had been praying about it and that he had received 'a word from the Lord' that it would be all right if they slept together. Like him, she believed that God could reveal his will directly, and yet somehow this didn't seem right...surely, the Bible said that it was wrong?

Have you ever been faced with this sort of question, ever been asked what Christians think about abortion, or if women should wear hats in church, or if homosexuality is a sin? Somehow it isn't enough to say glibly, 'We have the Bible, of course,' because Christians with the same Bible can come to different conclusions. And what about those problems which we have to face and which are not even dealt with in the Bible? Paul doesn't give us any advice in his letters about trade unions or strikes! How do we get guidance about this sort of thing? Well, this is what people mean when they talk about *interpreting* the Bible.

What are we after?

Interpretation (or as it is technically known, 'biblical hermeneutics') really tries to ask and answer two questions: 'What does the Bible say?' and 'What is the Bible saying to me, now, where I am?' This second question, of course, assumes that the Bible isn't any old collection of literature, but that although it was written ages ago, in some way it is meaningful for all generations including our own. We will discuss the reasons for that later. It is enough to say at this point that 'Scripture' has been used by Christians in living their Christian lives throughout the long and varied history of the church.

As we shall see, some are content with an answer to the first question. Interpreting the Bible for them is on a par with understanding any other ancient writings. They study the Bible as if they were going round a museum. Interesting and fascinating though this approach might be, it has little to do with our ordinary, everyday life. We say that they stop at an 'objective' understanding of the Bible. But for Christ and his disciples interpreting the Bible involved more than that. Their understanding of it had to be 'subjective' as well; relating Scripture to the individual and to the needs of every-day life – challenging and changing the situation. They regarded Scripture in this way because for them it was God's Word for all time.

But it is not always easy to see what the Bible means, and it is even harder sometimes to see what its teaching has to do with life today. How many young Christians have started to read through from Genesis to Revelation only to get bogged down somewhere between Exodus and Leviticus? How many have plunged into books like Ezekiël or Hebrews with the best will in the world, only to admit later that they didn't really see what the authors were going on about?

And yet it is vitally important that we do know what they were going on about and also what they are saying to our time. In fact, I would not be exaggerating if I said that this business of interpreting the Bible is one of the most important issues facing Christians today. It lies behind what we believe, how we live, how we get on together, and what we have to offer to the world.

Why our differences?

It comes as a bit of a surprise when we first become Christians to find out that while people believe the same Bible they can hold two different views about, say, baptism. Or that there can be widely differing emphases when it comes to God's sovereignty and man's free will. Or that there are seemingly endless permutations relating to Christ's second coming. All too often within the fellowship a great deal of heat – and not much light – is generated over issues like these. Christians who are otherwise delightful can argue savagely about charismatic gifts or prayer-book services and so on. There can be no doubt about their sincerity or about their equal commitment to the Bible. Some just cannot take it, and go off and join a denomination where all they have to do is to accept the official line. Most of us settle down to a bemused acceptance of this strange variety, never quite sure if we are believing the right things.

The disciples on the Emmaus Road were more highly privileged than they knew when the unrecognized Jesus began 'with Moses and all the prophets' and '*interpreted* to them in all the scriptures the things concerning himself'.[1] I wish I could have been a fly on the wall of the upper room when the risen Christ 'opened their minds to understand the scriptures',[2] but it can't be so. I am faced with understanding this remarkable book without having Jesus there, physically, to tell me all the answers.

I can hear someone saying, 'But don't we have the Holy Spirit instead?' True enough. But before we easily assume that this solves all our problems, it might be healthy to

[1] Luke 24:27.   [2] Luke 24:45.

8

remember that numerous scholars and ordinary Christians in every generation since Christ left have been able to claim this, and yet they have come up with some surprisingly diverse interpretations. We do not have to go very far to discover that the problem is still with us today!

So how do we tackle this problem? Well, to begin with, the Bible is certainly the proper place to start, but to ask *how* we are approaching it is very important too. This is the reason why Christians with the same Bible often get different results. It is not because they are dishonest or blind to the obvious. It is because they come to it from different angles. Sometimes they have carefully thought it through. Most of us, however, do it unwittingly because we unconsciously adopt certain attitudes. They are part of the traditions we have inherited or part of the mental atmosphere we all breathe.

Below the surface

We are not the first Christians to face these difficulties, even though we may think that our modern world is completely different from anything which has gone before. A good number of the questions which we will be asking have already been asked and answered in various ways. In fact, our modern way of life is in many respects the result of the past, and the ways in which we think are not really original at all.

This is why we are going to begin by looking at how Christians have tackled the job already. In this way we should save ourselves a great deal of time and possibly avoid some of the pitfalls into which others have fallen. More than this, in doing so we will ask ourselves *why* we think as we think and *why* we approach the Bible in the way that we do. We can then go on to work out some principles for understanding the Bible and applying it to life today.

Although we will be looking at some examples in passing, there are other books which get down to the detailed work of taking the Bible apart.[3] We are going to ask ourselves *why* we do what we do in Bible study. Let me put it this way. I'm a pretty poor mechanic, although that doesn't stop me driving

[3] See especially A.M. Stibbs, *Understanding God's Word* (IVP, 1976); P. Lee, G. Scharf and R. Willcox, *Food for Life* (IVP, 1977).

a car. I know about putting in the oil and petrol and keeping the water topped up. I can get around to tracing simple faults, but beyond that I'm stuck. My friend Fred not only drives his car, he knows how it works and *why* it does what it does. He went on a course and learned all about timing and sprockets and piston rings and tappets and such like. When he turns on the ignition he has a mental picture of what is going on under the bonnet. He knows what happens when he presses the accelerator or puts his foot on the brake pedal. Because of this, I am sure he gets far more out of his car than I do out of mine. And what is more, he's not at a loss when the thing breaks down.

What I am trying to do in this book is to take you inside the hidden machinery of understanding Bible truth. It will mean doing a bit of hard thinking. It will mean asking questions that might not have occurred to you before. It may mean unlearning some things which you have taken for granted. But in the end, my prayer is that you will handle God's Word with greater reverence – and with greater benefit not only for yourselves, but for others who come your way.

1
The story so far...

It is said of Oliver Cromwell that he wanted his son to learn 'a little history', no doubt because he realized that, although history does not exactly repeat itself, the same sort of issues do come up again and again. It is a pity that we have lost a sense of history. We sometimes give the impression that we are the first generation of Christians—and the cleverest—whereas a good number of able and spiritually-minded people had been at the game for a long time before we came on the scene. We need the grace to look at them and to learn from their attempts—and from their mistakes.

Even before the *first* Christians preached the good news, however, there was already a good deal of Bible in existence, and there were people who thought long and deeply about how best to understand it.

The Jews and their Bible

We need to remember that the Jews were 'a people of the Book' long before the Christians were. It comes as quite a surprise to some that the Bible used by New Testament believers was the Jewish Old Testament. It was rapidly supplemented by the New, but at the beginning it was their main source-book and teaching manual. Moreover, by the time of Jesus and the early church, the Jews had already tackled the problem of interpreting the Bible.

Plain teaching
They recognized, first of all, that certain passages of Scripture needed little explanation or interpretation: they spoke for themselves and could be taken quite literally. 'You shall love the Lord your God' means just that. When Jesus quoted it to

the Jewish scholars of his day, he didn't need to add a commentary, nor did they ask for one. The truth was plain and straightforward, and it still is today.[1] This did not appeal to some who preferred to chase up hidden and subtle meanings in passages which seemed to be quite clear, but for the mainstream rabbis it was quite adequate.

Working rules

What about those sections of the Bible which were not quite so transparent? How did they cope with verses or phrases which were difficult to penetrate? Over the years the rabbis evolved a number of rules designed to aid the Bible student. Later on these were multiplied to produce quite fantastic interpretations, finding meaning in peculiarities of grammar and style, manipulating the words and even the letters in the words—but as far as we can see, in Jesus' day they embodied a good deal of common sense.

For example, they saw, as we shall see, the importance of *the context* or setting in which a word or phrase was found. They were prepared to *compare harder passages with easier ones* on the same topic. They argued that the same phrase occurring in a number of different passages *was likely to mean the same thing.*[2]

Hidden meanings

Some were not content with the literal and obvious meaning of the narratives. As it was God's book they felt that they were entitled to look for 'spiritual' truths below the surface, and they did so by turning Scripture into a gigantic allegory like *Pilgrim's Progress* or *Paradise Lost*. People, places and events were supposed to represent spiritual, moral or intellectual truths. For example, Moses stands for intelligence; Enoch, repentance; Rachel, innocence; the five cities of the plain become the five senses, and so on.

As you can guess, the sky's the limit in this sort of approach, and the best qualification for an interpreter is a

---

[1] Mark 12:28-34 [2] For those who wish to follow this up, there are several books to help. The classic work on interpretation was for many years that of F. W. Farrar, *The History of Interpretation* (Macmillan, 1886), but modern summaries may be found in L. Berkhof, *Principles of Biblical Interpretation* (Baker, 1950) and B. Ramm, *Protestant Biblical Interpretation* (Baker, 1970).

fertile imagination. They actually borrowed this method from the Greeks who had used it to save the reputation of their ancient poets. What were often grossly immoral tales could be turned into moralizing lessons in this way. The peril is obvious. You can read out of the text what you first read into it—a temptation we still face.

Down by the shores of the Dead Sea there was a Bible-studying community which went even further in their claims. The rabbis applied their rules and argued, 'That has relevance to this.' The monastics at Qumran said, 'This *is* that,'[3] or in other words, they claimed that the Bible was finding its fulfilment in the events going on at the time. Moreover, they implied that not only the Bible but also their interpretation was God-given.

In the New Testament

Jesus and his followers were Jews, and therefore it is not really surprising that we find all the current Jewish ways of looking at Scripture in his teaching as well as in that of his disciples. We find them handling Scripture and pressing their arguments with it just like their fellow Jews. But there is something down-to-earth and common-sensical about them which prevented them from taking off on the more grotesque flights of Jewish fantasy. On the other hand, their claims are as radical as those made by the Qumran group and more so. They also saw Old Testament truths and texts finding their fulfilment in events going on around them.

For example, Jesus could say to the folk in his home town, 'Today this scripture has been fulfilled in your hearing.'[4] In the first Christian sermon at Pentecost, Peter announced that 'this is what was spoken by the prophet Joel...'.[5] And the rest of the New Testament writers continue, to a greater or lesser degree, in the same vein.

Christ the centre

But the most striking thing about the way in which they handled the Old Testament was that what had seemed

[3] R. Longenecker, *Biblical Exegesis in the Apostolic Period* (Eerdmans, 1975), pp.38-44.
[4] Luke 4:21.   [5] Acts 2:16.

previously to be diverse themes were now drawn together in a new and previously un-guessed-at unity.[6] They focused on Jesus Christ, on his origin, mission and destiny. Their message began with a statement about certain historic events which had happened 'in accordance with the scriptures'.[7] In doing this they were satisfying a variety of Jewish hopes in what must have been a startling way for those who first came to terms with the gospel. As one scholar puts it, 'The theologians of the New Testament make the same point as the historians. Christ was the end…of the Old Testament in the sense that he had fulfilled it and proved it true.'[8]

The same today?

How far can their principles for understanding the Bible be a guide for us? At times the teaching of Jesus and his followers is so geared to *Jewish* listeners that it might seem somewhat quaint to us living in the twentieth century.

Jesus, arguing with the Sadducees about the afterlife, cites the Old Testament phrase, 'I am the God of Abraham, and the God of Isaac, and the God of Jacob.' He goes on to imply that as God is a God of the living, these three must be alive somewhere and somehow.[9] Again, Paul sometimes uses allegory which, as we have seen, was more common in his day, but which does not have the same appeal for us.[10]

This in itself might be an example of how we must treat Scripture. As we will learn later, it must be understood *in its historical and cultural setting*, and the early Christians' setting was first-century Jewish. It is interesting that when Paul is defending the gospel in Athens before a Greek audience, he makes no attempt to use that sort of Jewish interpretation, or even to quote the Old Testament. In the synagogue at Antioch, however, his argument comes from Scripture and his use of the Old Testament is Jewish.[11]

Need for caution

When it comes to claiming that biblical predictions are being

[6] C. H. Dodd, *According to the Scriptures* (Fontana, 1965), p.109.   [7] *E.g.* 1 Corinthians 15:1-5.   [8] C. K. Barrett in D. E. Nineham (ed.), *The Church's Use of the Bible Past and Present* (SPCK, 1963), p.4.   [9] Mark 12:26.   [10] Galatians 4:21-31.   [11] Acts 17: 16-31; *cf.* 13:16-41.

14

fulfilled in our time we need to look at the lessons others have learned for us the hard way. Down the years, many have thought that they were qualified to interpret Scripture in this way and have done all kinds of weird and wonderful things as a result. For example, more than one group has announced that the Lord was about to return and, as a result, given away everything and gone to wait for him – only to return sheepishly bankrupt the next day! We also need to remember that Jesus and the apostles ministered under *special conditions*. They possessed a particular *authority* which enabled them to do what they did. It is highly debatable if we are qualified in the same way in our generation. Rather we depend on their ministry. We should really be trying to *reproduce* what they taught about God and the gospel. We are not called to do the job they did.[12]

How the church did it

It is a sad fact that, by and large, the church in the Middle Ages *did* follow one line of Jewish interpretive method. Very early on Christians began to look on the Bible as a gigantic allegory. Being positive, we might say that they were trying to understand the Old Testament in particular as *Christian* literature. Unfortunately, although they recognized the plain teaching of Scripture, they preferred to seek some hidden 'spiritual' meaning under the surface. In the early days, the major influence was the Greek education which many of the first Christian thinkers shared. Later on it simply became the accepted way of doing things.

Spiritual truths?
Who would have thought, for example, that Rebekah's meeting with Abraham's servant at the well really meant that we should come to the Scripture daily to meet with Christ? Or that when, according to Mark, blind Bartimaeus threw aside his cloak when he came to Jesus for healing, it represented the veil of spiritual blindness and poverty which he surrendered? Augustine tells us that the ark means the church; that being pitched within and without it is safe from

12 R. Longenecker. *op.cit.*, p.219.

15

inward and outward heresies. What is more, Noah's drunkenness is a picture of the death and passion of Christ!

Unfortunately this allegorical approach is not a thing of the past. I once heard a well-known preacher doing exactly the same with the story of Christ cleansing the temple. Because (he argued) the New Testament tells us that our bodies are the temple of the Holy Spirit, Christ has to drive all kinds of things out of our lives as well, if we are going to be completely given over to God. This is true, but not really what the account is all about.

Some were sane
In the old days there were voices crying in the wilderness. The theologians at Antioch rejected this approach and opted for the literal, plain sense of Scripture. They concerned themselves with what it had actually meant to the first writers and readers. (This is what we call the *grammatico-historical method* today and, as we shall see, it is very important.) Unfortunately, at the time, their views on other things were a bit suspect, and their influence was smothered as a consequence. Although individual churchmen used their method, it was the allegorical approach which was in vogue all through the Middle Ages and right up to the time of the Reformation.

Although allegory could be very helpful when used in Christian devotions – you can suggest all kinds of ideas very powerfully with pictures – it not only produced some outlandish results, it did worse. It propped up dubious church doctrines and practices. After all, the success of allegorizing depends on the sublety of the interpreter. If you are clever and imaginative enough, its possible to justify almost anything from Scripture this way.

The Reformation revolution
Although Christians had recognized the authority of the Bible before the time of the Reformation in the sixteenth century, it gained a new emphasis then. At that time a number of able people, whom we know today as the Reformers, became concerned about the low spiritual state of the church.

16

One of their starting-points was the idea that *God had spoken* to men and women. What is more, what he had said had been *accurately recorded* under the control of the Holy Spirit. Scripture was *'inspired'*. Consequently the Bible became *the only authority* for all that we need to believe, and for the way in which we should work it out in the church. Such a 'pre-understanding' is very important. Whoever we are, our interpretation of the Bible will largely depend on how we come to it. Our presuppositions (the ideas we begin with) in many ways dictate our conclusions. We see this working out in the way that they handled the Bible.

Plain and literal

Over against most of those who had gone before them, they maintained that it was the *plain and literal sense* of Scripture which was important. In other words, the Bible is not an allegorical puzzle to be solved by the ingenious. Martin Luther even called allegory 'monkey tricks'! Instead they opted for what we have called the *grammatico-historical approach*.

'Plain and literal' could be misleading adjectives for us today. As we shall see, it did not mean that they were clumsy, inflexible literalists with little imagination or literary sense. On the contrary they were indebted to a parallel movement called the Renaissance, which had placed great emphasis on the original texts of ancient literature and on the precise meaning of these texts.

Literature

This meant that they saw the Bible as literature. Appreciating literature means studying the languages involved, and the way in which those languages are put together. It means recognizing that ancient writers might have approached their task in different ways from those belonging to a later age. It means treating different *types of literature* such as historical narrative or poetry in their own right. It insists on the original setting, or *context*. John Calvin said that 'it is the first business of an interpreter to let his author say what he does, instead of attributing to him what he ought to say'.[13] No wonder his

[13] F. W. Farrar, *op.cit.*, p.347.

work still has value as we face that same challenge today.

The harmony of Scripture

Like the Jews before them, Christians were now also prepared to *'compare scripture with scripture'* to find its meaning. When they came across passages which were hard to understand, they would turn to others on the same subject to see if they might throw light on the difficulties. You can do this, of course, only if you accept 'the organic, theological *unity* of the Bible'.[14] If the Bible is merely a collection of diverse religious writings, we cannot expect agreement, nor can we legitimately use one passage to help us to understand another. If, however, while recognizing the distinct contributions of different authors, we also recognize one guiding hand behind their work, we may properly compare scripture with scripture and seek a harmony between them.

Christ the clue

The key to their way of understanding the Bible was one which we have already noticed in the New Testament writers' handling of the Old. It meant assuming that God had progressively revealed himself down through the years by many different agents, and that this self-revelation found its focus and completion in his Son (what we call a 'Christocentric' approach because it centres in Christ).[15] Luther, indeed, wanted to find Christ everywhere in Scripture. Calvin was somewhat more restrained, but both believed Christ to be the clue to interpreting the Bible.

The Holy Spirit

Starting with such convictions as these, it is not surprising that they also recognized that they needed *divine guidance* when they came to what they considered to be a divine book. They went further than that. Their understanding of God's grace in our salvation made them assert that, in their natural and fallen state, men and women cannot even begin to understand the things of God. To get at the true meaning of Scripture we need the help of the Holy Spirit who inspired it in the first place.

[14] B. Ramm, *op.cit.*, p.56.   [15] *E.g.* Hebrews 1:1-3.

18

They called this 'the inner witness of the Spirit', 'an illumination of the mind, or an opening up of the mind to see the truth, as well as a fixing of this truth firmly and securely upon the human mind'.[16] In this way God might make himself known to individuals while the professing church, lacking the essential experience, continued to live in error. They thus insisted on 'the right of private judgment'.

God's Word is final

One of their major concerns was to stand 'under' the Word of God, that is, not 'over against it', criticizing it or rejecting it. They maintained that the church should listen to the Word of God and conform to its stipulations rather than cutting Scripture down to her own size, picking and choosing at will. It was on those grounds that they felt able to take the church to task in their zeal for 're-forming' it. But the church could not take such criticism, and a sad history of division followed their efforts.

Half-truths

The story of biblical interpretation since that time might be seen as a series of one-sided distortions of their principles. Their work produced not one rival to the Church of Rome, but several, each claiming to represent the truth. This was the age of Confessionalism when ponderous statements of faith were constructed, claiming the support of Scripture, and generally aimed at some opposing camp regarded as not quite sound. As one scholar put it, 'They read the Bible in the unnatural glare of theological hatred.'[17]

Proof texts

What they did was to make a theological statement and then to undergird it with a series of biblical references. This 'proof-text' approach recognizes the authority of God's Word, but tends to take biblical statements out of their context. We all know how easy it is to misrepresent someone completely by quoting them out of context. Some journalists

[16] K. S. Kantzer in J. F. Walvoord (ed.), *Inspiration and Interpretation* (Eerdmans, 1957), p.132.   [17] F. W. Farrar, *op.cit.*, p.363.

in particular are highly skilled at it! As we shall see, the context is of immense importance when trying to understand what the text was intended to mean when it was first written. The grave danger of distortion is obvious. It would not be wrong to say that by a careful selection—and avoidance—of texts, it is possible to 'prove' most things 'from Scripture' without really representing scriptural truth at all, or at best producing a one-sided and unbalanced result.

It is in this way, of course, that modern sects collect a good number of their converts. When the Jehovah's Witness stands on the doorstep pointing out texts in the Bible to support his case, it seems fairly conclusive for a good number of people whose knowledge of Scripture is sketchy. If they had a bigger understanding of the book, they would see that often he was lifting verses out of their context and making them mean something quite different from what they meant originally.

Cutting to size

These dangers are not confined to sects or to those times. They are inherent in any 'systematic theology', that is, one which tries to collect and arrange biblical evidence in order to fit it into some over-all scheme. The strength of this method is that it provides a bird's-eye view of the whole of our faith. Its weakness is simply that it is just not possible to fit every aspect of God's revealed truth into any one human system. It is rather like trying to wrap up one of those awkwardly-shaped Christmas presents. Somehow the paper and string just will not go on neatly, and either you end up with bits sticking out, or you damage the goods in the process. So the rule is, 'Beware of the man with the over-neat package of beliefs!'

Nowadays scholars have seen the importance of the context in understanding what the Bible says, and this is one of the reasons why 'systematic theology' has fallen out of favour in some quarters. 'Biblical theology', the attempt to understand Scripture 'where it is', has been much more in fashion.

Making the right noises

Another by-product of this 'Confessionalism', as it was called, was a rather arid and intellectual assessment of the faith.

Orthodoxy came to consist in subscribing to the 'right' statements. Now this is true as far as it goes. We are told to 'contend for the faith which was once for all delivered to the saints'.[18] But Christian life and experience are much more than agreeing with our minds or even putting it into a form of words. I may recite the creed glibly on Sunday without it having the slightest effect on my life during the week, even though it contains statements of almost unspeakable wonder and demand.

A group in eighteenth-century Germany called the 'Pietists' were dissatisfied with that approach. They stressed instead the need for the Holy Spirit. Scripture has to live, if it is to be of any practical use, and only the Holy Spirit can make it come alive for me. It must be the Word of God 'at work in' believers.[19] There must be subjective response as well as objective truth. God's Word 'addresses itself not to the critical intellect alone, but to the whole personality, above all to the will'.[20] As Bengel, one of the best Pietist expositors, put it, 'Apply yourself wholly to the text; apply the text wholly to yourself.'

Blessed thoughts

This is all very true, but the practical result for many was a strongly 'personal' line of interpretation, the kind of thing we suffer from today in a good deal of 'devotional' writing and preaching. The words of Scripture can become merely the springboard for 'blessed thoughts' which might be true in themselves, but which often have little to do with the passage. Sometimes it is even the wording of a particular version which suggests the 'thought', and it falls to pieces with a different translation.

I recently heard a preacher announce as his text, 'Is it well with you, my brother?'[21] and I thought that we were in for some unusual insights into the lurid story of Joab's treachery. Not a bit of it. Instead, he went on to ask the congregation a series of questions about their spiritual health, 'How is your heart?', 'What about your hearing?' and the rest. In fact, it was good straight 'spiritual check-up' stuff, but it had nothing

[18] Jude 3. [19] 1 Thessalonians 2:13. [20] R. M. Grant, *The Bible in the Church* (Macmillan, 1948), p.170. [21] 2 Samuel 20:9.

to do with the text. He could have preached the same sermon from 'How do you do?' and not bothered with the Bible at all.

Having said all this, the positive contribution of the Pietists was that they stressed the need for the interpreter to be in spiritual harmony with the Bible author. As we shall see, this is essential if we are to get hold of the original concerns of those who wrote.

Liberalism

It seems ironical that the movement which began with the Reformers, and which resulted in the Protestant churches breaking away from the Roman Catholics, should ultimately produce scholars who would deny the very basis of the Reformation. Yet this is what happened. The liberalism of the nineteenth century, which destroyed confidence in the Bible for so many, was largely Protestant. And it began in Germany, the home of Martin Luther himself. Here we have yet another strange distortion of Reformed methods. It began with the 'plain and literal sense' of the Bible which, as we have seen, is quite legitimate.[22] The stream of Reformed thought was, however, joined by another which was essentially opposed to it. This was the humanistic movement in eighteenth-century Germany, called the Enlightenment.

This school began its speculation with an exalted view of man and his reason. God was shut out of a system which was basically anti-supernatural and where everything could be explained rationally. Its scepticism reduced much of the Bible to the level of man's religious gropings – often, it was claimed, expressed in forms unacceptable to a 'modern' and 'enlightened' mind. Everything was confidently judged by human reason. What could not be accepted intellectually was cut out or explained away in the light of the general religious development of mankind. Scripture often became simply a prop for current philosophy which, of course, changed with fashion as philosophies tend to do.

The results
Despite all its claims, the Bible was reduced to *a merely human*

[22] E. Krenz, *The Historico-Critical Method* (SPCK, 1975), pp.6-32.

book, or at best, the product of human religious genius, a collection of documents relating to ancient Israel and to a first-century Middle Eastern sect. Inspiration came to be expressed in Coleridge's principle, 'What finds me must have proceeded from the Holy Spirit,' or in other words, its power to inspire religious experience.[23] For in spite of what we might call an antiquarian interest in the Bible, a number of liberal scholars still professed the deepest reverence for the authority of Scripture. It was a curious mixture of scepticism and credence.

If the Bible is this kind of literary hotch-potch, we cannot seriously attempt to harmonize differences within Scripture, and the principle of comparing 'scripture with scripture' is also of little use. *We must expect contradictions* in a book written by a number of fallible and diverse human authors.

In place of unfolding, God-given revelation, human and often *random development* was a key theme in liberal studies. As time goes by, it was assumed, various streams of religious thought meet and mingle to produce new amalgams. A Bible author may be so strongly influenced by an outside and even alien system of thought that he may change the whole intention of the original message. To this day many assume that Paul was the arch-corrupter of the gospel who turned the simple moral teaching of the Galilean peasant-rabbi, Jesus, into a religion the latter never ever intended.

What is more, if the Bible books are only human works, then we must expect them to be *full of errors* like any other human writings; not necessarily intentional errors, but simply because of the limited perspectives of the authors. The canon of Scripture (the collection of the books as we have them) cannot be due to providence but to chance, and the works we have need not necessarily have been written by those named in them. So it became the great task of critical theology to bring order out of chaos. Unblinkered by the reverence of a worshipping church, they tried to sift through the biblical material in search of the 'original' Jesus or, if he was beyond recovery, the belief and practices of the earliest Christians.

[23] E. C. Blackman, *Biblical Interpretation* (Independent Press, 1957), p.131.

23

The reaction

How did Bible-believing Christians react to all this? Initially, apart from a few outstanding scholars, they beat a defensive retreat into an unquestioning acceptance of the Bible, no awkward questions asked. Unfortunately the inevitable equation: 'Bible-believing' (or 'fundamentalist' as they came to be called) equals 'obscurantist' (unenlightened) became the vogue. That is, it was the fashion to assume that belief in a God-inspired Scripture meant intellectual suicide; and sad to say, there were many whose attitude to honest scholarship endorsed that opinion.[24]

There were some who were prepared to tackle the claims of liberalism on its own grounds, but it has not been until recent years that Christians convinced that Scripture is both God-given and special (nowadays often called 'conservative evangelicals') have been prepared to learn from the results of modern studies, and to make their contribution at that level. How could they, when the roots of the movement seem to be so irreconcilably opposed to their fundamental beliefs? They have come to recognize that some of the questions asked by the liberals (and their present-day 'modernist' counterparts) were questions which needed to be asked, and that some of the issues raised had been long neglected. We have gained from the 'historical-critical' approach to Scripture, as it is called, a far better grasp of *the human element* in the Bible together with a deeper appreciation of its *historical sense*. Both of these dimensions are necessary if we are to interpret the Bible correctly.

They have also come to recognize that, although critical scholarship could and does produce wild and sceptical extremes, it can also establish surprisingly moderate and conservative results which are helpful in our understanding of the Bible. There are a good number of scholars who, while unable to hold to a thoroughly conservative evangelical position, nevertheless have a real respect for the Bible, and who are eager, within that framework, to discover what it has to say to God's people today.

[24] For a valuable discussion of this whole subject see J. I. Packer, *'Fundamentalism' and the Word of God* (IVP, 1958).

24

Unfortunately, whether it be the liberalism of the last century or the modernism of this one, the hallmark of critical scholarship has often been a sceptical approach to the biblical text. In practical terms it has made theology the domain of the experts, and has done a great deal to destroy the ordinary Christian's confidence in the Bible. In our universities and colleges, then in churches and schools, we have been taught that we can no longer trust the Bible and the ordinary person does not have the expertise to understand it for himself.

Coming to terms
On the positive side, conservative evangelical scholars are beginning to demonstrate their intellectual integrity by producing studies of high quality which are being recognized as such by non-conservatives. The fact that one can use critical tools and come to conservative conclusions means that faith in an inspired Scripture is not a throw-back from the past or a refusal to face the issues. However, some have issued stern warnings that handling critical material could lead to a denial of the Bible's inspiration. Some have felt that any traffic with biblical scholarship at this level is the beginning of the 'slippery slope' into modernism.[25] This is something of the tension that the conservative evangelical scholar experiences today. On the one hand he must be true to his commitment to the Bible as the Word of God; on the other he must be prepared to handle and assess the results of a scholarship which treats the Bible as little more than a human product.

Hard work for today
A good number of us came to trust the Bible without knowing anything about these technicalities. We did so for the simple reason that when we claimed the promises we found in the Bible, they worked for us. It was through this book that we came to a living relationship with God in Christ and by the Holy Spirit. Nothing, and that includes scholarship ancient or modern, can deny that. The Bible spoke to us and speaks to us, and all this business about interpretation seems to be

[25] H. Lindsell, *The Battle for the Bible* (Zondervan, 1976).

an unnecessary complication when it comes to living the Christian life.

Too much Bible?
In fact, we may even be tempted to react violently the other way, as some have done. We may have sympathy with the bewildered Christian who opts out when it comes to understanding the Bible for himself, or who takes refuge in 'spiritual experiences' which promise more direct guidance. Currently the charge of 'bibliolatry' (worship of the Bible) is laid against conservative evangelicals in some quarters. It is said that we have come to believe in a Trinity of Father, Son and Holy *Scripture*! History unfortunately illustrates repeatedly the chaos of sects and cults who felt that they could dispense with the Bible, and who ended up far, far from the truth. Unless the Holy Spirit contradicts himself, the revelation which some have claimed as immediate and God-given has been wildly astray from the original gospel message.

Think!
If we take the biblical gospel seriously there is really no alternative to the hard work of thinking through our position and its implications. As conservative evangelicals we claim to be the spiritual heirs of the Reformers. We claim to base our position on the truth revealed in the Bible as God's Word. We profess to put ourselves under God's Word, and to be open to what it might have to say to us in our generation.

In some respects we are highly privileged because we know much more about the Bible and its background than anyone who has gone before us. In other ways we have to start at the beginning and think through the issues for ourselves. We cannot do what some would like to do, turn the clock back and live in the past. But we can learn from the gains and losses of the past. We can take, and if need be adapt, the positive principles which have come down to us.

This is what we shall now attempt to do. We are going to try to forge a set of tools which will take us into the meaning of the Bible so that we may confidently go to it for help and guidance as we face the problems of today.

2
What does it say?

What about Genesis chapter one? Did God create the world in six twenty-four-hour days, or did he use evolution as his method over long and indefinite periods of time? Those who take the former line argue from the 'evening and morning' phrases; those who take the latter from the fact that 'day' does not always mean twenty-four hours in the Old Testament. But this is surely all beside the point when we ask what the original *intention* of this chapter was. What are we meant to learn here? Just this, that there is a God who created with infinite ease; that his creation was good; that man, who was the apex of that creation, was different in kind from the rest. The passage actually tells us nothing about God's *method*. It probably never occurred to the author to ask that kind of question. He *intended* other things.

What did they want to say?
This was the kind of question they began to ask after years of allegorizing the Scriptures away. 'What did the author mean when he first penned this?' 'How would the first readers have understood it?' Our first job is to try to get into the shoes of the original parties and see it from their point of view. In this chapter we are going to look at what we need to know if we are going to do just that, but before we get down to the nuts and bolts, there is a matter we have to clear up before we can move on.

Intentions
The question 'What did the author intend?' is no longer as straightforward as it might seem. It has been the fashion for some years now in literary circles to talk about the author's

intentions in terms of what motivated him, the personal experiences or circumstances or even state of mind which made him write as he did. If we read between the lines we are supposed to be able to discover these things.

This psychological approach to literature can almost become a form of allegorizing itself. We are told that we must not simply enjoy or appreciate the tale being told, but rather look beneath the surface for the personal implications. Hence *Alice in Wonderland* should tell us more about the Rev. Charles Dodgson's Victorian inhibitions than about Alice, and so on.

As always happens, there has been a strong reaction to all this. It has been recognized that too much literary and artistic criticism arises from *the imagination of the critic*! It is often highly questionable if the motives attributed to the author ever existed in his unattainable unconscious mind. There must be literary works where the author has no intention of revealing why he was writing, just as one can conceive of other occasions when authors were blissfully unaware of what made them write as they did. Again, there have been situations when the product has been certainly very different from the author's stated intentions.[1]

We have seen a similar movement among biblical scholars whose theories as to the origins, situations and structure of the Bible books have, at times, become unbelievably subtle. It ought to be warning enough that a good number of these hypotheses, some of which have dominated the world of biblical scholarship for a while, have fallen apart as fresh evidence has come to light, or simply as the fashion has passed. One suspects that a good deal of biblical criticism tells us more about the critic's mind, not to say his imagination, than it does about the authors of Scripture and what they intended. We need not be for ever hunting up complicated motives behind the writing of Bible books.

What sort of book?
How much we can actually know about a particular author's state of mind will depend largely upon the type of writing we

[1] R. Wellek and A. Warren, *Theory of Literature* (Penguin, 1963), pp. 147-150; E. W. M. Tillyard and C. S. Lewis, *The Personal Heresy* (OUP, 1965).

have before us. A highly personal, confessional letter such as 2 Corinthians is going to reveal much more to us about Paul than, say, 2 Chronicles is about its author, whoever he was. Although every historian has his reasons for writing (and that would include, for example, the authors of the gospels), something a good number of moderns cannot come to terms with is the fact that an author might be narrating an account simply for its own sake and not for some abstruse theological reason. As D. M. Baillie once said of the gospel critics, 'It seldom seems to occur to them that the story may have been handed on simply or primarily *because it was true.*'[2] One of the reasons for this is the deep, one might almost say pathological, scepticism with which some scholars approach the material.[3]

Written by people

To say that the Bible is literature has sometimes been to put conservative evangelicals on red alert for heresy! 'Surely', would come the rejoinder, 'the Bible is inspired', and inspired in a different sense from other so-called 'inspired' literature. (And they would probably quote 2 Timothy 3:16 into the bargain!)

A human book

All this is true – the Bible authors often claim as much themselves, as we shall see later. But at the same time, whatever the mystery and miracle of inspiration involved, the Bible did not drop from heaven on golden plates, nor was it dictated in some sort of heavenly typing-pool. Biblical inspiration means that God took up and involved the full humanity of the Bible authors as well as giving us a great deal more. So, in Paul's writings we *do* meet with Paul, and in Jeremiah's prophecy we come face to face with the prophet himself. God used real people with individual personalities which came across in their writings. Scripture is *both human and divine,* and if we are to understand it properly we must come to terms with both these aspects. Unfortunately in

[2] D. M. Baillie, *God was in Christ* (Faber, 1948), p.57   [3] For a useful discussion of this subject see C. S. Lewis, *Fern-Seeds and Elephants* (Collins, 1977), pp.104-125.

recent years, while conservatives have stressed the latter, modernists have concentrated on the former. Both positions are unbalanced.

We shall be looking at the Bible from the divine point of view later on. Concentrating for a while on the human side, we have to regard the Bible as a collection of writings in human language coming out from a human background, that is, as literature.

Literary styles

What is more, literature can be diverse in its expression, and the biblical collection is a good example of this. We not only have *narrative prose* (*e.g.* the gospels); we also have *personal letters* (*e.g.* those of Peter, John and Paul), we have *legal documents* (*e.g.* Leviticus) and we have large tracts of *poetry* (*e.g.* the Psalms)—to mention just a few of the different styles. Each of these will demand a different approach.

For example, in poetry there is a licence of expression and an employment of idiom which it would be fatal to understand in wooden, literal terms. (You try it with 'I wandered lonely as a cloud…' and see where it gets you!) This has now long been recognized to the point where most modern translations will attempt to print biblical poetry as poetry and not, as the Authorized Version did, in solid chunks of prose.

Fact not fiction

Let's not be guilty of making the mental equation: 'Literature equals fiction.' Some have argued this way, bracketing the Bible with other classic pieces of literature, good for us (like Shakespeare) because they form part of our cultural heritage. What is more, just as we recognize Hamlet and King Lear as imaginary figures, and think no less of them because of that, we must approach Abraham or David or Paul in the same way. It is true, of course, that the Bible has an undisputed place in western culture, but to say that the Bible is literature is not to say that it is not true or historical or that its characters never existed. It can contain fictional elements (for example, Jesus' parables are fiction) but it is literature in that it was written to be read.

A long time ago

A further complication when it comes to understanding biblical style is that its phraseology and diction are not what we are used to. The Bible is not only literature; it is ancient literature, with some parts more ancient than others. In fact, it would be better to talk about biblical *styles*, remembering that the earliest and latest biblical books were composed hundreds of years apart and in very different circumstances, not to say languages.

Different language

It is for this reason that it is very difficult to get an 'accurate' modern translation. In order to put the Bible into language which the modern man in the street can understand, the translator has to paraphrase, thereby inevitably, to some degree, losing touch with the original texts. This is why a good 'study' translation might not be the easiest to read.

For example, the Good News Bible, or even a version as racy as the Living Bible, comes over to us in ordinary, everyday language. This is not a bad thing. After all, the originals would have been in the everyday language of their own day. But they do this by paraphrasing to a greater or lesser degree the Greek, Hebrew and Aramaic in which the Bible was first written. That means that their translators have tried to find modern equivalents for phrases and statements in the old languages. For example, those who (literally) 'hunger and thirst for righteousness' become 'those whose greatest desire is to do what God requires' in the Good News Bible.[4] This reasonably represents the *ideas* in the text, if not the actual words. It is a different matter when the American edition of the Living Bible tells us that 'Saul went into the cave to go to the bathroom'![5] To get a little nearer to what the Bible actually said we need to go to something like the Revised Standard Version or the New International Version. The phrasing might seem more old-fashioned to the ordinary reader, but it often represents the original words more accurately.

[4] Matthew 5:6.   [5] 1 Samuel 24:3.

Different thinking

This leads us to another shattering discovery. The Bible authors did not just speak and write in languages different from ours; they *thought* differently from us. Every generation tends to ask different questions framed largely by the current philosophical outlook, the mental scaffolding in which they live and think. For example, there would be no question in those days about the supernatural dimensions to life. Everyone with very few exceptions believed in some sort of God or spiritual power, even if only superstitiously.

We must be aware of this when we come to the Bible. There must be what has been called 'historical distancing' between ourselves and such people as Isaiah and Luke, or we shall think about them as twentieth-century people.[6] Hollywood has not helped here. It becomes too easy to imagine Moses or Samson speaking with an American drawl! What is worse, if we are not careful we find ourselves reading our ways of thinking into Bible statements (Genesis 1 is a good example!), and expecting Bible authors to answer questions they never thought of asking.

We may also be tempted to think with the intellectual snobbery of the twentieth-century, and look down on all things ancient as being unsophisticated and naive. This despising of what is ancient or old in preference for what is new or young is a fairly recent idea. I have a friend who is always raving about the latest book or theory. I have often wondered just how we managed to live before it came out!

The man in his time

Something that we have to remember is that we are, everyone of us, children of our own time. Our standards, values and attitudes, in fact many of the ideas we take for granted, are largely the product of the culture in which we were born. If we are unaware of this, it will mean that all our thinking about the Bible will be distorted. We shall be reading it through twentieth-century spectacles.

[6] A. C. Thiselton in J. R. W. Stott (ed.), *Obeying Christ in a Changing World* (Collins, 1977), p.100.

Different culture

But the Bible authors were not twentieth-century Christians. Far from it. They lived in times and cultures very different from our own. At the same time these historical settings are not entirely beyond our reach. Historical studies can do a great deal to reconstruct for us the ways in which men and women lived and thought then. This in turn will help us to understand better both what and why they wrote.

It is this sort of background knowledge which throws a flood of light on, for example, Paul's instructions about women and their head-covering.[7] Although there are several difficulties in that passage, it has been argued that, far from being a sign of dutiful submission to the males, it was a mark of the woman's dignity and freedom as a Christian. In a situation where loose hair might mean loose morals, Paul is appealing for propriety or decent behaviour by the standards of the day. Otherwise the fellowship would get a bad name locally. Hats mean something entirely different today, and probably have more to do with the wife's control of her husband's cheque-book than with submission! Some have suggested that a modern parallel might be the custom of wearing wedding-rings. The wife's ring protects her from improper approaches, and marks her out as a married woman.

Archaeology

In this respect we are heavily in debt to that whole battery of scholars who have pursued biblical historical research. For example, biblical archaeology has opened up the world of the Bible for us, and has often cleared up difficulties in the meaning of the text. Some (*e.g.* Sir William Ramsay, who did pioneer work on the background of the book of Acts) have even convinced themselves of the accuracy of the New Testament evidence in this way. When he began his work he was very sceptical, but after he had actually examined the evidence he concluded that Luke was a painstaking and accurate historian.[8] For instance, his local knowledge of even

[7] 1 Corinthians 11:2-16.   [8] I. H. Marshall in I. H. Marshall (ed.), *New Testament Interpretation* (Paternoster, 1977), pp.126-127.

the different titles of town officials was confirmed by inscriptions which Ramsay unearthed.

Contemporary writings
Comparative studies, where the Bible is placed alongside other ancient traditions, have also been a great help. Whereas Bible authors may come close to very different conclusions from their pagan contemporaries, we must remember that they lived in the same world and used the same stock of ideas. This is why it is legitimate to turn to non-biblical writings of the same period as, for example, the New Testament books, in order to see how people thought in those days. We have a great deal of literature from the period between the Testaments, including the Apocrypha, which brings us up to date on the ways in which the Jews of Jesus' day had developed and had been influenced in their beliefs.

New revelation
We are not saying, however, that the New Testament is just another phase of this development. The writers were certainly not confined to their background, and they often transformed the ideas they inherited under what we believe to be the creative guidance of the Holy Spirit. But though they built their house to a different plan, they used the same bricks.

The effect of the discovery of the Dead Sea Scrolls is a good illustration of this. Whereas most scholars would agree that there is no direct link between them and the biblical writings, they use many of the same terms, phrases and ideas, which in turn help us to understand the ways that they are being used in the Bible. In particular these studies have made possible a completely different approach to John's gospel, which was long considered by many to be late and unreliable. The evidence of the Scrolls points the other way. The date could be early and the account is firmly rooted in eyewitness evidence.[9]

Help for us today
It is in ways like these that historical studies have often

[9] J. A. T. Robinson, *Twelve New Testament Studies* (SCM, 1962), pp.94-106.

endorsed the reliability of the biblical account or undermined theories discrediting Scripture. In the final analysis, of course, the only way to 'prove' the truth of the Bible is to live it, but in that such research has been an aid to faith, it has been highly valuable.

Fortunately, a good deal of this material is available to English readers in a variety of Bible handbooks, commentaries and encyclopaedias. This means that the ordinary Christian can build up a background knowledge of the Bible for himself. It is possible, of course, to derive a great deal of help and comfort from God's Word without it. The Holy Spirit makes Christ and the gospel known regularly to many who have no Bible background at all. If we are going to go further than the biblical ABC, however, and intend really to get a grasp of what the Bible teaches, there can be no short cuts. In this area, like all the others, there is no royal road to learning.

A book full of pictures

Having said all that we have about the medieval allegorizers, it is only fair to say that they touched upon a truth which is still a problem for us today. This is the fact that religious language is made up of ordinary terms used in a special way.

Human models

Thomas Aquinas recognized this years ago when he taught that when we speak about God we use *analogies*. We are really trying to express the inexpressible, for God and his ways are far beyond us and what we can put into words. So, taking some human model, we say that God is like this – but then again, he is different.

For example, when we use the term 'Father' of God we are using it in this way. There is much about the best of human fatherhood which we can credit to God, and yet even the best falls far short of his relationship with us. So we qualify the statement. We call him 'heavenly Father'.

(Sometimes, of course, this can cause problems for other reasons. I know a young girl who had great difficulty in getting hold of this particular truth because she came from a broken home where her father had been a brute to her. She had to learn what fatherhood was, seeing it demonstrated in Christian families she knew, before she could call God 'Father' with the love and confidence which that word carries for most of us.)

The Bible is rich in this sort of expression. Jesus called himself 'the Good Shepherd'; John the Baptist called him 'the Lamb of God'. In neither case do we think of him as a *literal* shepherd or lamb, although as they come in Scripture both these terms are full of meaning.[10] For this is the language of symbol where spiritual truths are expressed in pictures. 'The Good Shepherd' speaks to me of care, protection, guidance, nurture, discipline, and much else. The 'Lamb of God' sums up ideas such as innocence and sacrifice, sin and atonement, God's provision and man's need.

Apocalyptic

There is one biblical style which is almost studied analogy and symbol from beginning to end. This is the strange (to us) picture language of 'apocalyptic', the style in which the book of Revelation is written. Images drawn from Israel's history become symbols of spiritual truths, clear and inspiring to those steeped in the Old Testament, although something of a riddle to others. It might have been originally a sort of code language used to hide holy things from unbelievers in times of persecution.[11]

It would be perilous to understand it literally, although many have fallen into that trap. One bestselling author tells us confidently that 'the kings of the East' must mean Red China; that the nightmarish cavalry described for us in the book are nothing less than helicopter gun ships; that the sealing of God's people tells us that 144,000 literal, physical, Jewish Billy Grahams will be turned loose on the earth after the church has been taken away. This kind of thing makes fascinating sci-fi reading, but it has little to do with what the book of Revelation is saying.

---

[10] C. Brown, *Philosophy and the Christian Faith* (IVP, 1968), pp.30-32.   [11] L. Morris, *Apocalyptic* (IVP, 1973).

Real pictures

One school of thought argues that symbols and images are the clue to our understanding the Bible as a whole. Man, it is said, thinks about 'his own being, his world, his destiny and the objects of his worship' in terms of 'archetypal images', that is, pictures which answer to universal spiritual needs.[12] Most religions use pictures such as light and darkness, life and birth, death and resurrection, and the Bible is full of this kind of thing. So, they say, the inspiration of the Bible was not a matter of God passing on certain facts about himself, but rather giving the authors a series of symbols which express who God is and what he is doing. When we read the Bible, we recognize these and respond to them.[13]

This may seem a bit complicated, but there is some truth in it. The appeal of some Scripture passages is more poetic than propositional, and yet that is certainly not the whole story. The Bible does give us stated facts about God and man and Christ and so on which we can think about and grasp with our minds. It *is* possible to say 'what the Bible teaches…'. It is not just a matter of 'reality apprehended by the imagination', even though God's reality might be so big that it can be expressed only in symbolic ways and by analogies.

Furthermore, although religious language must necessarily be the language of analogy, the Bible claims that what it expresses actually happened in space-time, whether it was the exodus or the resurrection or what have you. Symbol maybe; but not fantasy fiction.

But I don't speak Greek!

The starting-point for all interpretation is naturally to come to terms with the basic material to be interpreted. With modern literature we often have the immense advantage of being in direct touch with both the language in which it is written, and with the original text of the work in question. Not so with the Bible. The Bible authors wrote in three different archaic languages – Hebrew, Aramaic and Greek – and without exception, we do not have the original texts of

[12] A. Richardson, *The Bible in the Age of Science* (SCM, 1961), pp.142-163.
[13] A. Richardson, *op.cit.*, p.161.

what they wrote, only copies of copies of copies.

Bible languages

These may appear to be insurmountable problems, but in practice this is not necessarily so. As far as the languages are concerned, we are better placed now than at any other time in history since those early days due to the long and painstaking efforts of scholars in this field. Although there are still tantalizing gaps in our knowledge, we have more understanding of the use of the words and phrases, and of the structure of those languages, than ever before.

A great deal of our insight derives from the fact that a large amount of non-biblical literature in those languages has come to light over the years which illustrates the use of biblical terms in different settings. For example, biblical scholars of the last century were restricted in their understanding of New Testament Greek, because all they had by way of comparison were Classical Greek works. Since then an enormous store of literature including books, bills and private letters, written in the same style as the New Testament, has been found. This, of course, has made some of the older scholars' conclusions out of date, but it has forwarded our current knowledge of what the Bible authors were actually trying to say.

Manuscripts

A similar thing might be said about the text of the Bible books. Here we have an embarrassment of riches. It may surprise some to learn that some of the ancient classical works are known to us by only a single, sometimes mutilated, copy. When it comes to the Bible, however, we have literally hundreds of copies as well as early translations into other languages. These latter put us in touch, at second hand, with even earlier editions. The discovery of early manuscripts over the last hundred years or so is an exciting story, and it is going on all the time. For example, when the collection of the writings of the Dead Sea Sect came to light in the 1940s, our knowledge of the Hebrew text of the Old Testament was pushed back about a thousand years nearer to the original almost overnight. (One of the remarkable aspects of these particular discoveries was that some of the Hebrew texts which turned up differed very little from modern editions which we were using.)

Copying problems

When work is copied by hand, as most of us know from personal experience, errors can creep in quite easily. The Bible texts that we have are the result of hundreds of years of copying by a variety of different hands, some careful and some not quite so careful. This has led to a large number of variant readings in the copies we have in our possession, although let us be quick to add that, as far as the bulk of the Bible is concerned, there is substantial agreement. In the early days of 'textual criticism' (as the study of these variants is called), scholars often worked by 'feel', accepting one manuscript as being fairly accurate and adjusting other readings to fit.

In recent years the study has become much more of a science and, by comparison and collection, what was the original can be established with a fair degree of probability. As with the languages, there are still gaps in our knowledge where different scholars fill in the blank or confused spaces in different ways, but none of these seriously affects the main stream of biblical truth.

Into English

The average Bible student will come to the job by way of translation, not knowing any or enough of the original languages to study at that level. Once again we have plenty of help as the last few years have seen a spate of modern translations in English. These may all be regarded as 'exegetical tools', that is, they can help us to understand what the Bible actually says. Many have had the happy experience of seeing the Bible come alive for them simply by reading the Scriptures in contemporary English. Passages obscured by out-of-date expressions in the older versions, or glossed over because we are so familiar with them, sometimes come across in a fresh light. It is useful to compare translation with translation, as the odd turn of phrase or emphasis may bring out the meaning of the text for us in a way we had not grasped before.

Alistair, a young science undergraduate, came to see me one day. He was deeply depressed, and was convinced that, although he thought he had become a Christian many years before, he had not been genuinely born again.

'There,' he told me, 'John says that "No-one born of God commits sin".[14] I sin, so I can't be a Christian after all.'

Of course, had he put that verse in the setting of the whole letter, he would have seen that John recognizes that Christians sin, and gives us tremendous reassurance that God will forgive.[15] So it could not mean what he thought. The clue here, however, is the original tense of the verb. John most probably meant that anyone who is really converted does not go on *habitually*, *repeatedly* sinning. If he lives like that, there is obviously no difference between him and an unbeliever. It was a pity that this incident happened before the New International Version came out. There it reads, 'No-one born of God will continue to sin.'

Get that text into context!

A text taken out of context, or so my teachers told me, often becomes a pretext. We have already seen that the weakness of 'proof-text' theology is that it can quite easily bend the original meaning of the passages. I know one good man who was fond of quoting in prayer meetings a verse which, in context, meant the exact opposite of what *he* did! And then there is that beautiful one in Isaiah often used to stimulate fellowship: 'Every one helps his neighbour, and says to his brother, "Take courage!"'[16] A great text, but the only problem is that the speakers are idolaters encouraging one another to trust in their gods! Or what about those choruses and songs addressed to Christ as 'the rose of Sharon' and 'the lily of the valley'? Has it never occurred to anyone that, in the love-song from which they were taken, it is the girl protesting that, compared with the other women at court, she was as commonplace and as ordinary as a daisy in the field?[17]

[14] 1 John 3:9.   [15] 1 John 2:1-2.   [16] Isaiah 41:6.   [17] Song of Solomon 2:1.

It is by taking texts out of context that you can quite easily make the Bible contradict itself. This is what Bill and Jane were doing at the beginning of this book. Both had taken their proof texts out of their original settings. Bill's verse, 'By all means save some', does not really justify his drinking habits. In context, Paul is speaking about giving up his rights and privileges in order to win others for Christ.[18] Whereas he does tell us that he was prepared to identify with people of cultures different from his own in order to do this, he is very careful to underline his responsibility to Christ when it came to his behaviour. What is more, when we look at the whole drift of his argument, he has some sharp things to say to those at Corinth who were compromising the gospel by their 'spiritual liberty'.[19]

At the same time, Jane was doing a similar thing with her verse.[20] The call to be separate from the world is quite clear, but we know from other things that Paul said that we should not cut ourselves off completely from our non-Christian friends.[21] Being a Christian does not mean living in a monastery!

The passage
All this adds up to the importance of the setting of a biblical statement. A verse taken from the Bible was originally part of a passage, sometimes a small section of an argument or description. Whereas some can stand on their own perfectly well without any distortion, a good number change in meaning – some slightly, some greatly – when taken out of that original setting. If we want to understand what a particular biblical statement means, we may have to ask what the whole book means if we are going to be fair to the author. Certainly we will closely study the passage in which it is found.

The words
A similar difficulty can arise from the wrong use of biblical words. It is sometimes assumed that every time a word

[18] 1 Corinthians 9:22.   [19] 1 Corinthians 10:23-33.   [20] 2 Corinthians 6:17.
[21] 1 Corinthians 5:9-10.

41

occurs in Scripture, it must have the same meaning. An added problem is that words develop and change in their meaning over the years. In the scholarly world, it had long been standard practice to trace the history of a term, seeking the way in which it had been used in and out of the Bible, and then to read that total meaning into a particular occurrence. We see a similar trend in some of our amplified translations.

In recent times, however, the absurdity of this practice has been pointed out.[22] What is important when understanding a passage is not what the word might have meant in earlier works, but how the author is actually using it there. The same words might mean different things in different settings. For example, Paul and James appear to be using the term 'faith' in almost contradictory ways. For James it means acknowledging facts about God; for Paul, it is often total commitment to God, practically 'obedience'.[23]

This does not mean that words mean nothing. They do have a stable core of meaning, but if we stop and think a moment, we never use them except in sentences or phrases where they are related to others which modify that meaning.

The ideas
Modern linguistic studies have thrown light on our use and abuse of biblical terms. From a linguistic point of view, a word is a written or spoken sound plus an idea or ideas to be conveyed by it. The sounds, of course, change with every different language. The ideas, however, may be related to others sometimes represented by different sounds. Traditional biblical word studies have concentrated on words of the same sound, form or root, and have often missed the fact that the ideas they convey might be related to those represented by other words. So in our word studies we should be looking for clusters of similar ideas – maybe represented by different terms – but which fill out and relate the meaning of a particular word in its context.[24]

Take a word like 'spirit' in the New Testament. In the

[22] J. Barr, *The Semantics of Biblical Language* (OUP, 1961).   [23] Ephesians 2:8-10; Romans 4:1-25; *cf.* James 2:14-26.   [24] A. C. Thiselton in I. H. Marshall (ed.), *New Testament Interpretation*, pp.75-104.

original it can simply mean 'wind', and there are several words for that in Scripture. Sometimes it just means 'breath' in a physical sense. It is also often used of the human spirit along with 'soul' and in contrast with the body or the flesh. Equally it relates to terms like 'heart', 'conscience' and 'the inner man'. It can sum up the whole person. But it is also used in a different way of God's Spirit, of his activity and power, as well as of other spiritual beings, angels, demons, principalities and powers, even ghosts. So you can see, it would be wrong to think that it meant the same thing every time. In fact it would be highly misleading.

All this might sound a bit technical, but it adds up to this: the only way of finding out what a word means is to study the context, the phrase, the sentence and the passage in which it occurs. Whereas it is useful to know what a word means in other situations, the immediate questions will always be, 'What does it mean here?' or 'How is the author using it at this point?' Some of our devotional books have completely overlooked this, and have worked more by sound than by sense. That well-used little guide *Daily Light* is a good example of this. Whereas there is sometimes a genuine theme linking the daily selection of verses, in other cases the only connection is some word which all the verses have in common.

Did they always know?

So far we have been arguing for recovering the meaning of the text when it was first written. How about those occasions when a writer's words turn out to mean considerably more than he originally intended? We can see this in the way in which New Testament authors sometimes used Old Testament texts. Was the psalmist in Psalm 2 originally speaking about Christ or about the current king?[25] Did Hosea really have a vision of Mary and Joseph's escape with Jesus into Egypt and subsequent return?[26] Then again, we have those great Old Testament pictures, or 'types', which are taken up and filled out in the New Testament gospel. Just look at what Hebrews does with Old Testament priesthood and sacrifice. Were these things really in the authors' minds

[25] Psalm 2:7; *cf.* Hebrews 1:5.   [26] Hosea 11:1; *cf.* Matthew 2:15.

when they were first described? Is that what they *intended*?

Things that come true

Now it is true that, at an ordinary secular level, our words sometimes have a way of fulfilling themselves in a manner we never intended, something which lies behind the popular superstition of 'Don't say that – it might happen'. We may put this down to sheer coincidence, of course, but could it just be possible that some events actually cast their shadow before them? Certainly we have occasions in Scripture when someone unwittingly predicted far more than they intended. Caiaphas the high priest is a good example of this, and John sees the hand of God in it.[27] Conceivably, in a similar way, some of the Old Testament prophets were not *fully* aware of what they saw and said, although their words no doubt had a meaning for their own time and place.

Prophecy

We might even regard their words as a sort of divine *double entendre,* so that although they might not have grasped the fuller implications, God knew and foresaw that later generations would see them 'like a teacher committing truths to children whose full content they will not understand till later'.[28] Some do not make much of the fulfilment of prophecy these days, but in New Testament times, particularly in a Jewish setting, it was a powerful apologetic or 'proof' of the truth of the gospel. If the gospel of Matthew is an example of the way in which they 'explained and proved' that Jesus was the Christ, they were working on the assumption that God could make the Old Testament mean more than one thing.[29]

Behind the modern dislike of predictive prophecy is the assumption that it is putting the effect before the cause in a 'cause-and-effect' world. How can we know something before it happens if the event is the cause and our knowledge is the effect? In this way scholars have had to explain away the 'precognitive' element in Scripture, when the writers claim to foresee forthcoming events. But is this really necessary? We

---

[27] John 11:49-52.   [28] R. E. Brown. 'The Sensus Plenior in the Last Ten Years', *Catholic Biblical Quarterly* 25.2 (July, 1963), p.265.   [29] Acts 17:3.

are now waking up to the fact that being aware of something before it happens is a far more common experience than has been hitherto admitted. Add the divine dimension and there is nothing improbable in the idea of God preparing the way for the gospel. In this sense, whether the prophets saw and understood or not, God was setting the scene for his Son.

Fuller meaning

To be fair, the 'fuller meaning' that New Testament authors sometimes see in Old Testament references is not really arbitrary, although it might seem that way to us. It is true that there is a difference between the historical king and his enthronement ceremony in Psalm 2 on the one hand, and the incarnation on the other. Yet at the same time there is a similarity, a line of continuity, between the two. The later truth, which the author may not have known, is closely related to the truth he did know; 'so that in hitting out at something like it, he was in touch with the very same reality in which the fuller truth is rooted.'[30]

We might add that it could be legitimate for us to use passages of Scripture in a similar way. Jesus' encounter with the woman at the well may not have been originally intended as a model of pastoral counselling, but to use the passage in this way would be entirely consistent with the original intention.[31] This is different again from allegorizing. We are suggesting an analogy where the same principles apply.

Take, for example, the story of David and Goliath. Very few of us are likely to be shepherd boys, almost certainly not on the hills of Palestine, and I would guess that none of us has had to fight a Philistine giant. Yet at the same time, there are abiding principles in what David did which are the same today as they were then. The big lesson, of course, is that of trusting God when we meet the challenges of life, and of proving God's protection and provision as we step out in faith. And we can probably think of other lessons which we can quite legitimately transfer from David's experience to our own.

[30] C. S. Lewis, *Reflections on the Psalms* (Bles, 1958), p.102.   [31] I. H. Marshall, in I. H. Marshall (ed.), *New Testament Interpretation*, p.14.

We must, of course, take care that our analogy really is consistent with the original, or we will be once again falling into the trap of fanciful allegorizing. As C. S. Lewis once said in this connection, 'What we see when we think we are looking into the depths of Scripture may sometimes be only the reflection of our own silly faces.'[32]

Types

'Typology' is similar, but somewhat different too. It is not simply seeing a profounder sense in Old Testament figures and events; there is often a contrast involved as well. Christ is our heavenly king in a way no earthly king ever could be; heaven is our spiritual Jerusalem; and so on. Once again we are warned by the misuse of this line of approach to tread very carefully, or we shall be seeing types and their corresponding 'antitypes' (as they are called) everywhere. It was said of one early church theologian that he saw the cross in every stick mentioned in the Old Testament! A good rule would be to ask if the parallel is warranted by the New Testament, and to confine ourselves to what the inspired authors saw and wrote. For example, in the book of Hebrews, the Old Testament system of priests and sacrifices is seen as having its fulfilment in who Christ is and what he did. But the writer does not go into detailed parallels between the blessings of the gospel and the furniture in the tabernacle or the high priest's clothes, as some later writers have done.

In our quest for what the Bible authors originally intended and what the book actually means, we have now gone one step further. We have been assuming that we are not just dealing with an ordinary book; that God had a hand in its composition. When we see the New Testament writers using verses in a fuller sense, or claiming Old Testament types to be fulfilled, we have to allow for the sovereignty of God in the whole operation. As we shall go on to see, when we deal with the writings of Scripture, we are looking for the divine intention as much as for the human.

---

[32] C. S. Lewis, *op.cit.*, p.121.

3
The book
that is different

That pioneer translator of the New Testament into modern English, J. B. Phillips, tells us that although he tried to remain emotionally detached from his work, 'I found again and again that the material under my hands was strangely alive'.[1] It was rather like rewiring an old house where the electricity had not been turned off! There was something 'uncanny' about the Bible books.

What is it about the Bible which makes it different from the other great works of literature? As we have seen it *is* literature, but is it more than just a human creation? What was it that drew this collection of assorted manuscripts together in the first place, so that Jews and then Christians claimed that it was one book and not many? After all, that is what they were assuming when they compared harder passages with easier ones when trying to understand them; that it was not just some books but *a* book, and then not just *a* book but *the* Book, God's book in fact.

There have been some who have claimed that it is unfair to come to the Bible like this. We ought to come, they say, 'with an open mind', confining ourselves to the objective study of a piece of literature. This sounds fine, but an 'open mind' is, in fact, a myth! When we start assessing Scripture, or anything else come to that, we all have certain ideas already in our minds, what we call a 'pre-understanding', which colours all our conclusions.

For example, as we have seen in the case of liberalism, if we do not believe in the supernatural, we shall set about explaining away anything which claims to be supernatural in natural terms. If we do not believe that God was behind the

[1] J. B. Phillips, *The Ring of Truth* (Hodder, 1967), p.18.

writing of the Bible, we shall look at it as a random collection of human literature.

What is 'inspired'?

Now it is reasonably obvious that what we call the Bible was originally a collection of books written by different people at different times. The result ought to have been diverse in the extreme, but both Jews and Christians recognized that they all had something in common. They believed that the Bible was 'inspired', that it was, in the final analysis, the product of the mind of God himself.[2]

When we speak about the 'inspiration' of Scripture in this way, we are using the word in a particular sense. We are speaking about that miracle whereby God took up the authors in the totality of their personalities, and caused them to write as they did. This is far more than inspiration in the usual literary sense of the word. When we say, 'The Bible is inspired,' we mean something rather different than when we say, 'Shakespeare was inspired,' or 'Tolstoy was an inspired author'. In their cases we are speaking about their literary genius which enabled them to write as they did. In the case of the Bible authors, we are claiming that God decided to commit truth about himself and his ways to objective written form, and that he used them to this end.

'Thus says the Lord'

This is certainly what they themselves claimed with almost monotonous regularity. 'Thus says the Lord' or 'the word of the Lord' are phrases that occur again and again in the Old Testament, and the New Testament writers assumed an authority which was no less. We may, of course, argue that a claim to inspiration in this sense does not necessarily constitute the genuine article. Many in the past, as well as today, have claimed that they were God's spokesmen, but their contradictory voices and lives have told otherwise. I know a fellow who claims to be a prophet in his own group. He *claims* to have a particular insight into God's will for the others, and

[2] See L. Morris, *I believe in Revelation* (Hodder, 1976); C. Pinnock, *Biblical Revelation* (Moody, 1971).

because they accept his claims, his word has become law. But somehow what he says and how he lives do not add up. I am not prejudging the issue of prophecy today; all I know is that the way in which this man behaves at times is considerably different from what I read about Christian leadership in the New Testament.

Christ as the key

The key to our understanding of biblical inspiration, the lynch-pin on which it all hangs, is a rather different person, Christ himself.

There can be no argument that Jesus assumed and built upon the idea that the Bible was inspired. In this respect he was one with the Jews of his own time. For him, the Old Testament recorded what God had revealed of himself to man, not simply in general terms, but in specific details. He could appeal to the very words of the Old Testament writers as having God's authority, and therefore as being above contradiction.[3] So, inspiration and Jesus Christ's personal authority go together. You cannot have the one without the other. When we say that Scripture is inspired, we are really only taking the claims of Christ seriously.[4]

Apostolic authority

One might say a similar thing about the New Testament writings. As with the Old Testament, the writers simply assume that what they have to say is God's Word with God's authority.[5] It seems that even in New Testament times some of their writings were given a status alongside the Old Testament,[6] and the very collection of them tells us that Christians rapidly became 'a people of the Book' like the Jews before them. For the early believers these books and letters spoke with the delegated authority of Christ as did no others – and there were others to choose from, some bearing the names of apostles who were supposed to have written

[3] For example: Matthew 4:4,7,10; Mark 12:35-37; Luke 4:16-21; John 10:34-36; *etc.*
[4] See detailed discussion in J. W. Wenham, *Christ and the Bible* (IVP, 1972).   [5] For example; 1 Corinthians 14:37; 1 Thessalonians 2:13; 1 Peter 1:23-25; 1 John 4:6; *etc.*   [6] 2 Peter 3:15-16.

them. There was a vibrance and a vitality about the twenty-seven which we have today which attracted support from Christians everywhere. These were the books which spoke to them in the same accents of Christ himself.

Was Jesus wrong?

Some have argued that the whole idea of Scripture is unnecessary for the Christian faith.[7] Others have tried to maintain that Christ's attitude to Scripture was simply part of his self-limitation; that in becoming man, the Son of God became human to the point of being a child of his own time, limited in outlook so that he accepted what to us are unacceptable and dispensable ideas. But this is to question the very basis on which the Christian faith is built. If Christ was wrong on this point – and he seems to give considerable weight to it – how can we be sure that he was right on any point?

We are left to our own subjective devices, selecting what appeals to us from Christ's teaching and the Bible generally. In a word, we construct our own religion and way of life, but it cannot be said that we have taken Christ and his authority seriously.

Modern views

The bane of modern theology which has largely dispensed with the idea of inspiration is its sheer subjectivity. Read half a dozen different theology books and you end up with half a dozen different gospels or even half a dozen different Christs. Some aspect of the New Testament message which may appeal to one man as important carries no weight at all with the next. This then filters down through our colleges to our church pulpits and RE lessons where preachers and teachers tell us that 'it may be this or it may be that. The scholars are not agreed'. As a result, the ordinary person does not know who or what to believe.

I am not unaware of the many problems involved in understanding the Bible, but, along with a good number of

[7] A. C. Thiselton, in I. H. Marshall (ed.), *New Testament Interpretation* (Paternoster, 1977), p.114.

others, I prefer simply to start with Scripture and the idea of inspiration where Christ did.

Let us not be so naïve as to think that we are the first generation which has seen difficulties in approaching the Bible in this way. The Jews themselves were also quite aware of a good number of the Old Testament problems, and yet they tenaciously held on to the divine over-ruling and consequent authority of those writings.

God's Son

In Christ and his absolute claims to authority, we have an endorsement of their views which we can dispense with *only if we dispense with him*. In insisting on the inspiration of Scripture, conservative evangelicals are confessing that, difficulties and problems notwithstanding, they will follow Christ.

To argue the authority of the Bible from the Bible in this way has seemed to some to be a circular argument. 'Why do I accept the authority of the Bible? Because the Bible says it is authoritative!' But this is to misrepresent the situation. We need a higher authority to validate its claims. The ultimate authority, of course, is God, and if Christ is God's Son as he claimed to be, that authority comes down to us through him and his teaching.

How do we know that Jesus was (and is) the Son of God? Not just because he or his followers might have claimed that to be so, but because God raised him from the dead. Now if you read what the New Testament teaches about that, you will find that the writers are not simply making a bald claim, but rather that they invite us to consider the eyewitness evidence for ourselves. The resurrection can be investigated historically. The apostles did not believe and preach that Christ had risen merely because they had somehow got the idea into their heads. Something had happened to them. They had seen Christ alive after his death. When Jesus was executed, they were broken men. They had nothing more to live or hope for. When he rose from the dead it revolutionized their whole attitude to life as well as marking him out from the rest of mankind.[8] What is more, it validated all his

8 Romans 1:3-4.

claims, which in turn provide a point of reference for any other claim to authority, including that of Scripture.

Little by little

Another important presupposition lying behind this particular approach is the contention that the Bible has *one theme*. Despite its detail, it tells from start to finish of God's saving action in Christ. The Old Testament prepares for his coming; the New Testament expounds it. This is no new idea. Augustine back in the fourth century said as much, and he was only reiterating the claims of the New Testament writers themselves, that the Old was being fulfilled before their eyes.[9]

A growing light

This introduces us to something else that we must bear in mind when we interpret the Bible. God did not reveal himself and all his ways at one go. God's self-revelation to his people was like light dawning and growing fuller as the years went by. We call this 'progressive revelation', and it is something of a safeguard. Whereas we can compare scripture with scripture, it must be in the context of a God-directed development. This is why, for example, it would be totally wrong to expect Abraham or David to behave as Christians before the time. They lived long before the revelation was complete. What is remarkable is that they lived as well as they did with the little light that they had. At the same time, what God did in them and through them prepared the way for the fuller revelation which was to follow. Hence Abraham's faith and David's deep spiritual longings both find their fulfilment in the New Testament Christ.

This does not mean that we are excusing the inconsistent behaviour of such people as Abraham and David. The Bible characters are described for us 'warts and all' as the fallible human beings that they were, and I am sure that God intended it that way for our encouragement! When evaluating their stories, we have to distinguish between what is simply descriptive and what is actually prescriptive or commanded. Sometimes what they did is an example to us of

[9] For example,1 Peter 1:10-12.

'how not to do it'. I am told to follow the example of Abraham's faith but not of his polygamy! The unhappy effects of the latter tell me that he was adrift at this point.

When talking about 'progressive revelation' we must also be careful not to confuse it with the popular view of religious development, that of man's 'long search' for God. This is the evolutionary view of religion, which makes out that man has been seeking after spiritual realities, in terms of crude and primitive ideas at first, but ultimately refining his views into higher beliefs.

I had an RE master at school who confidently told us that all religion had evolved from animism and spiritism, the worship of the spirits, to polytheism, the worship of many gods. From this it became henotheism, which has one high god plus several others, and eventually monotheism, the worship of one god, which is were we were at! His conclusion, of course, was that Jesus and the Christian faith were just the latest step on the evolutionary ladder, which did not please those of us in the Christian Union one bit. Later on I came to learn that this approach underlay a good deal of the liberal estimate of Jesus in the nineteenth century. For many, then, Jesus was just the greatest and best believer who ever lived, the man who found God, and so on.

God steps in
Not only does this theory about religion fall down through inconsistent evidence – some very primitive peoples hold relatively high views of spiritual things – it turns the idea of 'revelation' on its head. From a biblical point of view it is always God who takes the initiative, stepping into history, coming and revealing himself to man in his need.[10] Unaided, man may express his longings and fears and may reflect something of the fact that he was originally made in God's image,but he can never come to God through his own efforts. Progressive revelation is not the story of man's religious development, but the account of God's successive dealings with man, leading him out of his blindness and into the true light.

Anyway, for the working evangelist or minister all this talk

[10] Galatians 4:8-9.

about men and women groping after God seems like a bitter joke. It may be true in some parts of the world, but in my experience the ordinary chap in the factory or the office generally could not care less about God. If anything, when confronted with spiritual realities, they run away rather than clamour for the truth. That kind of reaction has more to do with the Bible view of revelation than with religious evolution.

One book or many?

This idea that there is one theme as far as the Bible is concerned is not accepted by many modern scholars. For example, one has maintained, 'The unity of the New Testament is a problem only because of the dogma of a holy book.'[11] Partly because of the stress on the human side of Scripture, the fashion has been to talk about biblical theolog*ies* rather than biblical theolog*y*.

This means that we cannot say 'what the Bible teaches' on a particular subject, but only how Paul or John or some other writer saw it. Because we have a collection of books from a number of minds, almost as diverse as the local lending library, it is argued that they must inevitably diverge and disagree. Hence John can be set against Paul, Peter against Luke and so on.

Parts of the same picture

Now there is no question about the plural authorship of the Bible, nor can we overlook the fact that different authors expressed themselves in different ways. That, however, does not necessarily mean that they have to disagree with one another. It is equally possible to argue that their individual teachings are complementary, that they round out one another.

Truth is many-sided, and different situations such as those confronting the authors and prompting their work demanded a stress on different aspects of the one truth. There were times when God's people needed comforting, as we discover in many of the psalms; equally there were times when they needed warning, which is what we find in Amos or Malachi. There were those who needed to be reminded that salvation was by

[11] C. F. Evans, *Is 'Holy Scripture' Christian?* (SCM, 1971), p.34.

r. Or you may bend over backwards to try
one with the other. But not only is it difficult to
armonize, it is equally irresponsible to dismiss
er out of hand. The fact is that our data a
, whereas those who wrote the accounts sto
ly nearer to the event than we do. We ma
but when all is said and done, we have to adm
not know for certain how things worked out.

cals find it very hard to do this. They have been
ys to have an answer for any and every question
t come their way. It is hard for them to say, 'I just
.' We need the honesty and humility to acknow-
there are many things we do not understand at

e ever wrong?

doubt that, for Jesus and the apostles, Scripture
itative because in some undefined manner it was
its very wording. The way in which they were
pin their arguments on the words themselves,
merely on the general truths contained in the
dence of that. For them it was wholly trustworthy
very words as a source of information about God
ys with men. The Reformers adopted the same
ripture was 'infallible' in that it never misled or
e honest inquirer. The negative side of this
ositive assurance is, of course, that there are no
the Bible: that it is inerrant.

tion

sense in which we must qualify the Reformers'
ter all, an infallible source does not necessarily
n infallible interpretation. We have seen this
ated for us in the acrimonious debates of the
l era when, as heirs to the Reformers, all the
accepted an infallible Bible. It is a little naïve to
we all believe in an infallible Bible, we shall all,
, come to the same theological viewpoint.

faith, as did the Galatians; there were others who needed teaching that faith must express itself in works, as the readers of James' letter. We also need reminding sometimes that some of the books in the Bible were written in far from ideal conditions. One wonders if some of our modern scholars would be quite so comprehensive and consistent if they had to do their work in prison or on some hazardous journey.

Only one gospel

To set the Bible authors against one another is really to overlook their own sense of oneness in their fidelity to what God had revealed to them about himself. When it came to the gospel, Paul could claim, 'Whether then it was I or they, so *we* preach and so you believed.'[12] Equally he could castigate any who veered from what he knew to be God-given truth.[13] The New Testament authors were not writing tongue in cheek when they spoke of '*the faith*' (not '*the faiths*') which was once for all delivered to the saints. They meant it, and if we are going to take them seriously, we must accept that in good faith.

Their job was to make Christ known. So we find them, each in his own way, passing on the same message, not a different one.

What about the problems?

All this is not to say that there are no problem areas when it comes to interpreting the Bible. On the contrary, with the Bible being – in human terms – a collection of writings addressed on particular occasions to men and women far removed from our time and culture, it is to be expected that at times we shall have difficulties in grasping what the authors wanted to pass on. Of course we can be so preoccupied with the problems that we can forget that there is plenty in the Bible which hardly needs interpretation. The message is clear and relates to human needs just like our own. There are also areas, texts and passages, however, with which we must grapple if we are to understand them.

[12] 1 Corinthians 15:11.   [13] For example, Galatians 1:6-9.

Start with the obvious

As we have seen, we might find help in some cases by studying clearer passages on the same subject. To ask, 'What is Jeremiah saying at this point?' may be answered by asking, 'What else has he said on the same topic elsewhere?' Knowing what he has plainly taught on another occasion will mean that there are certain things which he *cannot* be saying, while at the same time it might throw light on our difficult verse or passage. With the proviso we have mentioned about different authors sometimes using the same word in different ways, we may similarly move from book to book within the canon.

For example, a good number begin their study of the second coming of Christ with the highly symbolic book of Revelation. It would be much wiser to start with those clear and unambiguous statements about Christ's return which we find elsewhere in the New Testament, and then to try to understand Revelation in the light of them. If we fail to do this we might find ourselves constructing our doctrine from obscure and difficult texts. This is what the Mormons have done with their practice of baptizing on behalf of those who have died. The verse they use to support this teaching is obscure in the extreme.[14] Nobody can yet be completely sure of what it means. What they do, moreover, is inconsistent with the plain statement of the gospel both in Paul's writings and elsewhere in the New Testament. Whatever it means, it cannot mean what they have taken it to mean, that is, that you must be baptized if you are going to be saved, and that if you are not, then someone else must be baptized on your behalf.

Set the scene

As we have seen, sometimes the answer to a biblical riddle comes from outside Scripture as we learn from some extra-biblical source something of the background against which the Bible was written. The temptation in this approach is to assume that the biblical writers must have reacted in the same way as their Jewish or even pagan 'opposite numbers'.

For example, the problem of Paul's personal background

[14] 1 Corinthians 15:29.

as long divided New Testament s
he Dispersion, reared in Tarsus c
nfluences to which he consciously o
his gospel? Or was he true to his J
may understand him better again:
Old Testament and rabbinic thou
clearly claims the latter position, a
opted for the former, even mainta
Christian faith was set on a course o
originally intended. When we actu
Paul's writings, however, we find
pagan background could provide. '
quite explicit, that God had done a
that the Christian gospel was nei
nor borrowed paganism. While
which has provided us with a k
climate of Paul's day, we must no
something original when he choos

When in doubt…

It is also a great temptation, w
difficulty, to fill out the gaps with o
the possibilities and to disregar
remember that conjecture is only o
personal revelation. When weig
involved in interpreting an obscure
feel that one explanation is more p
is perfectly legitimate if we reme
with probabilities and not certain

At times it takes more courage t
agnostic, to say that we do not ur
yet. That 'yet' is important, becau
of the last 100 years that countless
cleared up, not to say many hyp
evidence has come to light. A 'su
thing and may be the wisest cours

Take, for instance, the two a
death.[16] You may, of course, conc

[15] Matthew 27:3-10; *cf.* Acts 1:18-19.

are in err
square the
how they
or the ot
incomplet
considera
conjecture
that we do

Evange
reared alw
which mig
don't kno
ledge that
present.

Is the Bib
The source
There is n
was autho
inspired in
prepared t
rather tha
Bible, is ev
down to th
and his w
attitude. S
deceived t
essentially
mistakes ir

The interpre
There is a
position. A
guarantee
sadly illus
Confession
combatant
think that
of necessi

Conservative evangelicals today are united in their confidence in Scripture, but divided over such issues as baptism or covenant theology or the second coming of Christ. Our interpretation of even an infallible Bible will depend on our background, experience, prejudices and expectations.

Inerrancy

The whole subject has recently come to the foreground of theological debate among evangelicals. They have asked again in what sense they can use terms such as infallible and inerrant for Scripture today. In some circles infallibility has generally been taken to mean inerrancy. Some, however, would argue for an infallible Bible which was not inerrant, a position sometimes called 'limited inerrancy'. As far as the great truths which are central to salvation are concerned, the Bible, they say, is infallible. But because the Bible authors were conditioned by their own contemporary world views, they wrote things which we know now are not true.[16] The other wing have replied that the Bible is not only without error in what it teaches, but also in what it touches. Hence we must pay attention to its descriptions of man and the universe, even though modern science would explain them rather differently. If it is true at one level, it must be true at all levels.[17]

Is it possible to speak about an inerrant Bible? It largely depends in what area you are asking that question. For example, when it comes to textual studies, for all the work that scholars have done, as we have seen, in places it is still impossible to reconstruct the original with total confidence. Again, when it comes to style, the authors' use of their language ranges from the very good to the far from perfect. We could not use the Bible as a textbook for perfectly regular Hebrew, Aramaic or Greek grammar and syntax. (Try reading the Greek of Revelation!)

Science and the Bible

It is, however, at the so-called 'scientific' level that the battle has raged. How can we, with our twentieth-century views of

[16] S. T. Davis, *The Debate about the Bible* (Westminster, 1977).   [17] H. Lindsell. *The Battle for the Bible* (Zondervan, 1976), p. 18

the universe, derived from observation and research, abandon these views in preference to those which appear primitive and mistaken? In some respects this is only an aspect of the 'science versus religion' debate which has raged ever since T. H. Huxley crusaded Darwin's views against the church. It has led to the popular belief that science has disproved the Bible, despite the fact that in practice a good number of scientists are also Bible-believing Christians.

What is sometimes forgotten is that scientific language is descriptive, and that it reflects the limited viewpoint of the observer. The man with the electron microscope is going to describe the universe in a rather different way from the man who sees it only with the naked eye. But this does not invalidate the latter's conclusions. How many of us living well into the post-Copernican era still speak about the sun *rising*? We ought to talk about the earth rotating! Yet we know perfectly well what we mean, and from the point of view of an ordinary observer, the sun *does* rise. In that sense it is a perfectly valid description.

Scripture, like any other ancient document, contains what we can call archaic scientific descriptions. They are not necessarily invalid or erroneous; they are limited by the point of view of the observer. What is more, they are generally secondary to the message of Scripture. The Bible was never intended to be a handbook on astronomy, medicine or Hebrew grammar.

There is no inherent contradiction between pure science and religion. The one describes the universe as it finds it; the other explains it. The problems sometimes arise when the scientist turns philosopher and begins to explain the universe in a materialistic or mechanistic manner.

Do the accounts conflict?
A similar thing might be said about another area in the debate, the alleged historical discrepancies in the Bible. Take the resurrection appearances of Jesus. As we have said, those who saw him shared their experiences, and it is these that we have recorded for us in the gospels, Acts and Epistles. That they did see him, eat with him and talk with him comes

across quite clearly, but it is not quite so straightforward when we try to piece the story together, asking the question, 'Who saw him when?' Our difficulties are largely due to the fact that we lack the viewpoint of the original observers. Even eyewitness accounts will often vary in detail, not because the individuals concerned were necessarily mistaken or self-deluded, but because different aspects of the event either appealed to them or were hidden from them. It is just not adequate, when faced with seemingly contradictory reports in the historical sections of the Bible, to dismiss one or both as in error. From their respective viewpoints, they may both be right. Even a secular historian will look for ways of harmonizing apparent discrepancies, including the possibility that his own interpretation might be wrong, before judging the text as mistaken or deliberately misleading.[18]

This is why evangelicals have traditionally attempted to reconcile, for example, the gospel records or the books of Kings and Chronicles where the data available appears to be divergent; the so-called concordist approach. Changes sometimes happen because of what the author is aiming at. So details are sometimes omitted because they are irrelevant. The order may be changed because the chronology of the event may not be the most important thing for us to know. And, of course, we have to remember that history sometimes does nearly repeat itself. 'It is a poor historian...who immediately accuses his sources of error and distortion on the assumption that *similar* incidents do not happen, rather than weighing up what is the most realistic explanation of the accounts as they stand.'[19]

This approach is infinitely more reasonable than that of the scholar who seizes on any apparent contradiction in order to dispose of the trustworthiness of the documents, rather like a lawyer disposing of hostile witnesses. Unfortunately some appear to reverse the dictum of the law-courts: 'Innocent until proved guilty.' It is the responsibility of the Bible historian to question the text in order to find out, as far as he is able, what exactly happened. It is quite another thing

[18] R. T. France, 'Inerrancy and New Testament Exegesis', in *Themelios* 1.1, Autumn 1975, p.16.   [19] R. T. France, *op.cit.*, p.16.

to approach the text with a scepticism which disbelieves anything until it can be proved true. As Prof. Howard Marshall says, 'In the absence of contrary evidence belief is reasonable.'[20] We were not there, and they were, or at least they were much nearer those who were.

Asking the right questions

It could be argued that, even if there were no debate about the trustworthiness of Scripture, 'inerrancy' would be the wrong word to use when we come to literature. It may be perfectly justified when applied to a telephone directory, but literature seems to be in a different category from this.

Style

It is in the essence of literature that the author has licence to use a wide variety of literary devices – words, phrases, allusions, conceptions – in order to achieve his end, and which he might never have intended to be taken at their face value. Every culture has in its linguistic inheritance a vast number of forms derived either from its own history or borrowed from other cultures, which have lost their original literal meaning, but which readily convey ideas. Our own language is full of them. If we were to be as wooden and unimaginative in our interpretation of English literature as some require us to be when handling Scripture, the result would be laughable.

In this respect it is of immense value to study the literary types (or *genres*) of the Bible authors' contemporaries when they are available to us. For example, although the New Testament writers turn the style of their letters to their own end, they do follow the basic epistolary form of their own day. They begin with a greeting, a thanksgiving and a prayer just like other letters of that time.

Facts and figures

Part of our problem might be that we are coming to the Bible with the wrong set of questions, questions which it was never intended to answer. They arise out of our own particular

[20] In I. H. Marshall (ed.), *New Testament Interpretation*, p.134.

cultural and philosophical background, and make us force ancient literature into a twentieth-century mould. Those who wrote the books of the Bible were not always as concerned about the details which we have come to look for. They were not always as preoccupied with trying to present facts objectively as we are; they were just as interested in what they meant spiritually. They came to their subject with a trust in God and a confidence in the gospel which dictated a positive approach. Their concern was for the great truths which the world needed to know in order to be saved, not the exact numbers of Israelites killed in a battle or even the exact order of events in Jesus' ministry. As we have already maintained, their whole philosophy of life (and that includes the way they handled history) was somewhat different from our own. It was not inferior because of that. They were children of their day, most certainly; but we are children of ours, heirs to a godless generation which has exalted man and his reason. In our conceit we assume that we are right and they were wrong, but this is not a foregone conclusion.

Overdoing it

It is not only Modernists, who do not necessarily believe that the Bible is inspired, who fall into this trap. Evangelicals are sometimes just as guilty of asking the wrong set of questions. While it is not unreasonable to believe that the Bible accounts do not contradict one another, efforts to reconcile the details sometimes become ludicrous. One recent author, worried about the apparently differing records of Jesus foretelling Peter's betrayal, ended up with the cock crowing on not one or two but four occasions! It was the only way in which he felt that all the evidence fitted in. It did not seem to occur to him that the writers were probably far more concerned about Peter's fickle allegiance to Jesus than they were about the habits of Palestinian poultry!

Under God's Word

The reason there was a Reformation was that individuals felt that in the Bible they had found God's revealed truth, and that they had to submit themselves to that truth. The Bible in turn became 'the touchstone of truth' as they called it. Everything had to be weighed and measured by the Word of God, even religious traditions of long standing. If other views differed from the Bible, it was God's Word which pronounced judgment and not vice versa. In terms of life and belief they put themselves *under* the Word of God. 'Let God be true though every man be false' was, for Calvin, the fundamental basis of all Christian thinking.[21] So convinced were they of this principle that even their approach to Scripture was conditioned by Scripture. Their 'pre-understanding' of the Bible itself was biblical. What do I mean by this?

The Bible by the Bible

Dr Jim Packer has pictured this process of interpretation as a spiral.[22] First the interpreter must go to the text of Scripture to learn from it the doctrine of Scripture. He must ask, as we have done, how Christ approached Scripture. From this understanding of the Bible, he then works out his rules for interpreting it. He then returns to the text of Scripture, applying these principles in order to understand Scripture better. This in turn will tell him more about the sort of book the Bible is. In the light of this he then adjusts his approach and returns to the text and so on. The method can be seen as a one-way system: from the biblical texts to the doctrine; from the doctrine to the method of interpretation; from the method back to the texts again. So by successive approximations, which Dr Packer calls 'a basic method in every science', the interpreter moves progressively closer to the truth underlying the text.

Thinking biblically

Many of our problems in interpretation arise from the fact that, although we may be professing Christians, we do not think biblically. With the hindsight of history we can see that even the Reformers were not entirely consistent. They also were indebted to their own times and culture. But if they failed it was not their fault, for it was certainly their intention

[21] Romans 3:4. [22] 'Hermeneutics and Biblical Authority', in *Themelios* 1.1, Autumn 1975, p.6.

to rediscover and apply biblical principles to every department of life. On the positive side, they did produce a whole new world-view, which has been only slowly eroded over the years and of which traces still remain in western culture.

The challenge to us is to do a similar thing in our own generation. Unfortunately we unconsciously accept the values, standards, outlooks and methods of western atheistic materialism. Take, for instance, Christian parents' ambitions for their children. How many want their offspring to get a 'good' job (= well-paid), with 'decent prospects' (= promotion and more money)? How many have woken up to the fact that in biblical terms it does not matter what they do, where they go or whom they marry *as long as they are in God's will*? How many really believe that 'godliness with contentment' is 'great gain'? Or that the materialism of this age can be 'a snare'?[23]

But then it is just as possible for us to come to the Bible with reservations about the supernatural. We have been reared to think in that way. Our generation has sanctified doubt. When I first learned in Sunday school about the miracles, it was with the rider that 'God does not do things like that nowadays'. No wonder we get such a shock when he does!

Ironically the spiritual vacuum which this has created has left us open to a pop existentialism which encourages us to live by the tides of emotion and to trim our attitude to God's Word by the feelings of the day. We have to 'feel led' before we get on and do anything. We talk about our 'experiences' – by which we mean how we felt at the time – and our 'problems' – by which we mean times when we do not feel so good. It really has little to do with being a Christian. It is simply the spirit of the age in which we live.

We can never finally free ourselves from this kind of thing, but we can try to bring our attitudes under the judgment of the Word of God. The world-view which we assume to be the only one may be far removed from the way in which God wants Christians to think. We need the grace – and the courage – to go to Scripture and face its teaching squarely instead of explaining it away. We need men and women who will dare to put themselves *under* the Word of God once again.

[23] 1 Timothy 6:6-10.

4

Are you tuned in?

So far we have been looking at the Bible as a book, and yet, at
the same time, we have recognized that it is more than just *a*
book, that it is God's Word. As we have come to realize, this
means that we cannot just think of it as a museum piece. It
has something to say to us today, even though we live in a
very different world from the one in which it was written. So
our next question must be, 'How does the Bible speak to me
today?' 'What has it got to do with my life at home or in the
office or on the building site or wherever?' But first of all we
have to face up to a difficulty which is simply due to the way
in which we have been reared to think.

Written to be lived
One of our greatest drawbacks is that we live in a tradition
going right back to the Greeks which values knowledge for its
own sake. A good deal of our western educational thinking is
based on the unquestioned assumption that it is a good thing
to 'know', without necessarily asking what we can do with
what we know. I met a student a little while ago who con-
fessed blandly, 'Of course, the degree I am reading qualifies
me for nothing,' except presumably to teach others the same
subject! Now we have been told that this is not a bad thing,
that this is 'education', and that it makes us much more
interesting and fulfilled people. Hence we can accept the
phenomenon of 'the unemployable graduate'!

We see the same trend all through the history of Christian
doctrine as well, where the chief end of man has often been
regarded as being the defining of religious truth. To frame a
comprehensive creed or confession, or to explore the fine
differences between theological statements, has been seen at

times as a major aspect of the church's job. It became a fine art in the Middle Ages, when theologians debated at length about how many angels could dance on a pin-head, or whether or not Christ could have come as an ass and not as a man! But then we can find the same attitude around today. When my young friend Peter was newly converted, he went along to his college Christian Union, eager to get on with the job. All he found, he told me later, was 'a group of Christians sitting in a circle discussing the Bible and theology *and doing nothing else'*.

Preaching and practice

Now it is quite clear that the Bible authors often set out to instruct. It was not that truth did not matter; it mattered a great deal. But truth without life, knowing without doing, is a sterile product, and no concern of prophets or apostles. While the western church has been inordinately proud of its theological theorizing, the biblical saints were much more concerned with *doing the truth*.[1] The Bible was written to be lived. It is not merely a theological manual; it is a handbook about godly behaviour.

The real test of theology is what good it does. The 'successful' theologian is not necessarily the one who gets his PhD in some abstruse subject, but the one whose work builds up the church and leads others to faith. Perhaps we might have avoided a great deal of unproductive scrapping between denominations or groups or schools of theology if we had been a little more pragmatic in our attitude to God's Word – and to other Christians.

Somehow we have to bridge the gap between 'What does it say?' and 'What is it saying to me today?' or 'How does it apply to my life?' After finding out what it means (what we call 'exegesis'), we have to go on to see how it comes to bear on practical situations (sometimes called 'exposition'). We must begin with solid exegesis, but we must not stop there. Some preachers do stop, and thereby miss the point of preaching. They might tell us, for example, all the ins and outs of God's dealings with Abraham, without showing us

[1] The literal translation of John 3·21

67

how to trust God for ourselves as Abraham did, or how God's promises all those years ago are fulfilled as we get out and make Christ known to others. A Sunday congregation needs from the pulpit something to take to work with them on Monday. True biblical interpretation is no spectator sport.

It answers back!

It is possible that parts of the Bible were not necessarily written to be taken apart and minutely analysed. They could have been written simply to have an impact on the hearer or the reader; they were written to stir the conscience and stimulate the will; they were written to move men and women to action.[2] If this is so, we shall not really understand such passages until we have been moved and stirred and stimulated ourselves. Let's remember that the Bible is what the Communists would call a 'dialectical' book. It argues with you! It cannot leave you unchanged or unchallenged. Your study must inevitably prompt your obedience or provoke your hardening.

A good example of this is Jesus' teaching in parables, when he used words to build an imaginary world which involved the hearers in a personal way (we even have some of their involuntary reactions recorded for us in the gospels). The result was that his teaching became part of their immediate experience, and did not remain as cold, dead fact on the slabs of their minds. Or read some of the Old Testament prophecies and try to imagine how the first hearers must have felt!

Worship

For a similar reason Scripture and scripturally-based hymns and prayers have long formed an integral part of Christian worship. When we hear the old truths read, said or sung in that context, we are *moved* to praise and penitence, thanksgiving and commitment. Let's not confuse this with mere aesthetic experience when something beautiful – a view, a piece of music, a picture or a poem – might 'move' us. A true

[2] A. C. Thiselton in I. H. Marshall (ed.), *New Testament Interpretation* (Paternoster, 1977), p. 114.

experience of worship has to do with fundamental truths about God and man and their relationship in Christ.

To say that the Bible is great and moving literature is not an excuse for neglecting the truth it contains. We really appreciate biblical literature only when we respond to its *message* with our wills. But in order to do this, something else has to happen to us.

Not on our own

If you begin, as the Bible does, with a high view of God in all his majesty and holiness, you will inevitably come to a lowly estimate of yourself and your need. This is the background to what we know about God's grace. Salvation is free for the simple reason that God has to do it all. We are in no position to help ourselves, and our helplessness extends to this whole area of knowing, let alone doing, the truth.

Modern man, generally, has a far more optimistic view of himself and his own abilities than this. He has been conditioned to think that he is quite capable of finding his own way in the world, and that having found it, he can follow it. He assumes that what he basically needs is knowledge, and that he can come to that knowledge by his own effort and application. Humanistic religion says the same thing. The teachings of Christianity, it has been argued, like those of many another faith, are really man's attempts to live a life well adjusted to himself, his neighbours and his environment.

Along with a good number in my own generation, I was taught in Sunday school that being a Christian was a matter of 'following Jesus' example' or 'being kind to others' or 'living by the Sermon on the Mount'. (I had not read it at that time or I would have given up in despair!) Christianity, as a result, became equated with a rather innocuous middle-class respectability.

Wanted: a miracle

This is a complete parody of the teaching of Scripture. In biblical terms man is not only a sinner because he sins; he sins because he is a sinner. His problem has to do with his very nature. Because of this, he is incapable of even understanding spiritual truth by himself, let alone living it out.[3] In New Testament terms there has to be a miracle, when God acts in the individual's life, a new creation, for him to see and live. The unconverted man, however clever, educated or imaginative, cannot understand spiritual truth for himself. He is blinded by Satan, and the gospel is sheer stupidity to him.[4] We can appreciate spiritual things only by the Holy Spirit. We need a God-given insight which is part of being regenerate or born again.[5]

New light

A biblical gospel relates to the whole person. Far from being confined to the assurance of forgiveness, wonderful though that might be, it involves a new and God-given potential for life. Regeneration is not merely self-reformation; it is God himself doing a work at the very roots of our personalities, 'in the heart', by the Holy Spirit. Among the effects of this are a new understanding and appreciation of spiritual things. We begin to 'see' truths to which we were previously blind. We are amazed that we did not see them before, and we are perplexed by the fact that our old friends do not see them as clearly as we do. We become alive to issues to which we were formerly dead; they begin to matter to us as never before.

This is why, in practical terms, the Bible becomes a new book to us when we are born again. Previously we either never read it or failed to see that it was relevant. Now when we read it – and we want to do so – it speaks to us and our immediate needs. When we hear it preached, it strikes a chord deep within us. We begin to understand the psalmist's enthusiasm when he wrote, 'Oh, how I love thy law! It is my meditation all the day.'[6]

The Holy Spirit

This being the case, we cannot interpret the Bible properly if we have not been born again. The person who lacks this experience, be he ever so well read and highly educated,

---

[3] For example: Jeremiah 17:9; Isaiah 64:6; Matthew 15:18-19; 1 Corinthians 2-14; 2 Corinthians 4:4-6; Ephesians 2:1-3; Romans 8:7-8; *etc.*   [4] 2 Corinthians 4:4; *cf.* 1 Corinthians 1:18-25.   [5] John 3:1-12.   [6] Psalm 119:97.

cannot appreciate the spiritual truth in Scripture as it was meant to be understood. The Holy Spirit is the interpreter *par excellence*, and without his aid we cannot grasp what Scripture really intends. To put it another way, the born-again believer sees God's truth from the inside; the unre-generate man, scholar or no, is on the outside looking in. He cannot see things from the same perspective.

Conservative evangelicals have traditionally majored on this experience. Much of their work in the world has been concerned with proclaiming the good news and stressing the need for men and women to come to a personal commitment to Christ (hence 'evangelical', from the Greek *evangelion*, good news). They have discovered that this experience, together with their common appreciation of the Bible as God's Word, has given them a basis for fellowship and co-operation which has crossed traditional denominational boundaries. In practice, their united activities have usually found expression either in evangelistic ventures or Bible-teaching conventions, both focusing on the Word of God.

What price scholarship?

How does all this affect the way in which we view the work of biblical scholars who might not profess such an experience? Does this mean that their work is valueless? Not necessarily so, because there is a good deal which may be studied and researched about the objective form of the Bible which is accessible to everyone. A knowledge of the biblical languages, for instance, or a study of background or introductory material, does not depend on spiritual experience. These subjects can be approached in the same way that we might deal with maths or geography. In that sense and at that level all biblical scholarship may be of use, and it is precisely at that level that conservative evangelicals have sometimes been lacking in the past. They have looked on spiritual illumination as a short cut which exempted them from the hard work of biblical research. But valuable as it may be, such study is not enough on its own, and when we move from the form to the content of Scripture, the born-again believer has an immense advantage.

71

This is simply because we recognize that like will understand like; that to understand fully what someone is trying to say, we need what we call 'an existential rapport' with that person. That is, we need to stand where he does and see and feel things the same way. For instance, only those who have been bereaved can really sympathize with the bereaved; only those who have suffered can really get alongside the suffering, and so on. Now those who profess to be born again would claim that this has been brought about by the same Spirit who indwelt and inspired the New Testament writers. In other words, their experience is of the same order, and in that respect they are in an unparalleled position when they come to understand the first authors.

Part of the negative reaction to 'modern scholarship' is that this perspective is so often lacking there. It is evident from the way in which some scholars handle Scripture that they are not really in sympathy with its message. For example, their explanation of the miracle – not to say the miracles – of Scripture is often humanistic, lacking an appreciation of what the Holy Spirit can do in a life, or even reflecting a refusal to believe. Their work, though valuable in some respects, will often leave many with a sense of frustration, even anger, that people should presume in their cleverness to do such things with the Word of God. I must admit that I sympathize with the man who wrote to his newspaper complaining that he was sick to death of hearing theologians and churchmen on television 'sharing their learned doubts'.

The last word?
Does this mean those who are born again say all that there is to say about the Bible, and that their interpretation is infallible? No, once again, because they are still sinners being saved. In fact, they ought to be the more ready to confess that they know only in part, and that God's ways are immeasurably higher than man's understanding. If, however, their Christian experience is genuine, they do possess a viewpoint which they share with the authors of the Bible who likewise have committed their lives, through faith, to God and his

Son. In a particular sense they share the ultimate concern of the writers. For them the Bible cannot be just an ancient book or an interesting book. It is the Word of God which speaks to human situations and needs today just as it did when it was first written.

The Bible speaks today
In the hundreds of years which have passed from the time when the Bible books were written to the present day, whole civilizations have come and gone. We find ourselves far removed in the ways in which we think and live from the first readers. In what sense, then, can we claim that the Bible speaks today? By any estimate much of its advice appears to be out of date and geared to an entirely different world from our own.

For example, the Old Testament laws about idolatry and polytheism may still be relevant in some parts of the modern world, but how does this affect those of us living in the West in what seems to be a post-religious (not to say post-Christian) secular climate of thought?[7] Or, how do Paul's lengthy discussions about what Christians felt they could or could not eat, in the first century, have any bearing on practical living in the twentieth century? 'Meat offered to idols' may still have a decidedly contemporary ring in some cultures today, but it hardly excites a flicker of recognition, say, in Britain or the USA. One might extend these objections to include the whole mental outlook of the biblical authors. Their entire world-view was so different from ours. In what respect, then, may I go to Scripture expecting it to speak to the needs and concerns of my own generation?

Myths?
It may seem strange to some that this has been the concern of a number of scholars who, though wedded to a negatively critical approach in biblical scholarship, still believe that the Bible has a message for today, if only we can extract it. Some have used the rather difficult idea of 'myth'. By this they

[7] See, for example. J. A. T. Robinson, *Honest to God* (SCM, 1963); A. Richardson, *The Bible in the Age of Science* (SCM, 1961).

understand the way in which people look at the world; the intellectual framework, the very thought categories of a generation which causes its members to speak and write as they do. In spiritual terms it is 'the use of imagery to express the other-worldly in terms of this world, and the divine in terms of human life, the other side in terms of this side'.[8]

Whereas the biblical writers used such symbols, we use different ones; we have different 'myths' which are part of the modern world in which we live. There is, theoretically, no suggestion that either the ancient or the modern myths are superior. It is simply a recognition that we think in different ways and that we ask different questions, or at least, if they are the same questions, we couch them in different terms.

If this is the case we must begin with 'demythologization', or the separation of the essential truths from their mythological framework. Then these in turn must be 'remythologized' into categories which modern man can appreciate. The motive behind this approach is the perfectly sincere attempt to translate the Bible into terms which modern man can grasp.

Looking for principles
There is a sense in which this is not new. Christians have always recognized that they must go behind the statements of Scripture to the *principles* underlying them. We may or may not face polytheistic idolatry today as the Israelites did, but, without too much trouble, we can see that the Old Testament prophets were appealing for an undivided devotion to God and a spiritual worship. In the same way, I may not face a crisis of conscience over meat offered to idols, but I still have to deal with the insidious influence of the world which comes to me through many an 'accepted' western practice. I also have to deal with the issue of doing things in different ways as it arises from the cultural gap between young and old, or East and West, in a modern church fellowship.

An older Christian lady once complained to me that, although a good number of younger people had started going to her church, they came to the services in what she called

[8] R. Bultmann in H. W. Bartsch (ed.), *Kerygma and Myth* (SPCK, 1953), p. 10.

'boiler suits'. She had been brought up to go to church in her 'Sunday best'; the youngsters, many of whom had no church background at all, were turning up in their jeans and sweaters, and thinking nothing of it. My older friend was offended because the young people's style of dress ran counter to what she had been brought up to regard as proper and respectful. It was not a matter of the youngsters going against scriptural teaching, for, as we know, the Bible does not stipulate what clothes we must wear when we go to church to worship. This lady had simply been reared at a time when views on dress were very different. In the same way the Gentile and Jewish Christians in Rome or at Corinth came from vastly different backgrounds, and had to learn to live with one another. Paul's advice – 'demythed' and 'remythed' maybe — fits the situation like a glove.[9]

Or take another example. When the Bible authors spoke about God's otherness in terms of distance – God above and the world below – they were using terms that I understand quite easily. The Russian cosmonaut's assertion, that there was no God because he had been up there and had not found him, only makes us smile. But let's remember that this is because we have mentally de- and re-mythologized biblical terminology.

Today's questions

Of greater concern is the extent to which some modern scholars feel that they can strip the teaching of Scripture in order to reach what they think are the underlying truths. How do we recognize them? Modern man, they have claimed, does not talk about God, sin, atonement and so on, but he is very concerned about his *existence*. He continually asks himself why he is here and what the world is all about; what we call 'existentialism'. Hence we must translate the biblical teaching into language like this if we are going to communicate with him. To do this, we must enter into debate with the Bible about our human existence. I go to the Bible with my question, and receive an answer which makes me revise its original terms. I then return to the text and ask again, and so

[9] 1 Corinthians 8-10; Romans 14:1-15:7

on. It is not just a matter of asking the questions. The Bible tells me how I should ask them.

Eternal truths
People today are certainly looking for some real purpose in life, but is that the whole story? They may be asking why they are here, and expressing their disillusionment with the world as they see it, but *ought* they not to be asking about their sin and their estrangement from God? It is right that we enter into a debate with the text of Scripture, but we must be careful to remember that the Bible always talks about man *in relation to God*. If we are not, we shall conclude that, because modern man does not ask about these things, they are therefore unimportant. We shall be in danger of the old error of forcing our ideas upon the Bible, rather than allowing the Bible to judge us and our ways of thinking.

The tendency in modern theology is to be man-centred. Instead of talking abut God, Christ and the gospel, the biblical characters are pictured as talking about their existence or their humanity or, when the principle is pushed to the extreme, simply about themselves. At bottom it seems like another expression of the 'long search' approach to religion, the difference being that man does not find God at the end of the trail; only himself. What is more, the great revealed truths of Scripture, not to say Christ himself, easily become symbols of the way in which we understand ourselves rather than God's reaching out to sinful mankind.

Of course, God does use modern man's questionings about himself to bring people to faith in Christ. I know a young man who got to a college of education only to feel that life had no purpose at all. In his disillusionment with the world he turned to Christian students who told him the answer. But he had to learn that the real problem had to do with his sin, and that the real solution was to get right with God by trusting Christ.

Indeed, the whole idea might be misguided. Is it really true that modern man cannot understand the words that the Bible uses? As Professor F. F. Bruce puts it, 'For those not familiar with the vocabulary of existentialism, talk about inauthentic and authentic existence is not more intelligible than the

Pauline vocabulary of sin and grace, law and liberty, retribution and acceptance, estrangement and reconciliation.'[10]

I was a minister in a downtown London church when Bishop John Robinson's bestseller *Honest to God* hit the market. Here, it was claimed, we had a sincere attempt by a leading churchman to update the language and message of the gospel so that modern people could understand it. I can well remember the perplexed lady who came to me clutching her copy and asking, 'What does it all *mean*, Mr Balchin?'

Getting involved

Some groups of modern scholars would go even further. They would say that the Bible writers were not just trying to instruct their readers, but to move them to some sort of personal response, some 'moment of truth' about themselves. We have already seen that Jesus did this sort of thing with his parables. His hearers got so caught up with the story that they reacted in all kinds of ways. If we are going to do the same for our own generation, we need to do more than just turn the Bible into modern English. We must put the message in such a way that it will involve our hearers.[11]

In many ways this is the old debate about subjective and objective truth. It is not enough to have a row of cold statements about God. I must be personally involved. When I come to Scripture I must not only ask what I can learn from the text, but what difference it makes to me. The truth must be truth for me, personally, and must affect every area of my life.

As we have seen, this is all correct. But we must be careful lest we go one step further and say that unless truth is truth to me it cannot be truth. As far as the Bible is concerned, it most certainly can. Whereas Scripture does engage and challenge in the ways suggested, there is also a great deal of straight teaching, historical claims, argument, all of which calls upon us to *think* and not just to react.[12] God's truth remains true whether we have encountered it for ourselves or not. It

---

[10] In I. H. Marshall (ed.), *New Testament Interpretation*, p.52.   [11] This whole approach has been called 'The New Hermeneutic'. See J. M. Robinson and J. B. Cobb (eds.), *The New Hermeneutic* (Harper and Row, 1964).   [12] A. C. Thiselton in I. H. Marshall (ed.), *New Testament Interpretation*, pp.308-333.

remains true even when we have rejected it. It will judge us whether we believe it or not.

Getting it across

On the positive side this whole approach does remind us that people in different cultures do think in different ways, and that because of this we have need of a 'cultural' as well as a verbal translation. But there is nothing very new in that understanding. The process was going on in biblical times. When Paul said that he was prepared to become all things to all men that he might by all means save some, he meant just that. We see it well illustrated in his letters, for there we have a Jewish gospel in the process of being translated into the thought forms of a Greek world. The miracle was that he and others did this with no loss of content.[13] We tend to throw out the baby with what we consider to be the bathwater.

For there is all the difference in the world between translating and transforming. Translation is the ever-present task of the church. On any showing, however, one particular group of scholars have done the other thing and transformed the gospel out of all recognition. As before, the challenge is to do better if we are to communicate with people in our own time. We must remember that, from one point of view, the gospel will never be *acceptable* to modern man or any other kind of man, if we are true to its terms. The message of the cross always offends some – it did when it was first preached.[14] But at least we can attempt to make it *intelligible* to modern man, including modern Christians who share the same intellectual background of their contemporaries.

When I prepare to preach I try mentally to sit alongside the ordinary members of the congregation – Bill the lorry-driver, and Jean the nurse, and Keith the teacher – and ask myself how it will come over to them. Not only is theological jargon a foreign language to them, but they will often miss the force of some of the simplest Bible terms, because they live in another world. If, for example, I want to teach them about redemption, I have to paint a word-picture of what it was like to live as a slave, and what it cost to set him free. But

[13] G. Dix, *Jew and Greek* (Dacre, 1953).   [14] 1 Corinthians 1:22-23.

78

then I must go on and tell them that this is what Christ has done for us, and that this means that he can give us the power to kick that sinful habit or free us from the dogging anxiety and so on. It must relate to their world and their lives; to their jobs and to their kids; to inflation and to the awkward neighbour next door. It must challenge the godless, materialistic conditioning which is coming at them daily from all angles, from the television, from advertising and from the magazines they pick up. It must lead them to think biblically, that is, in God's way, about the world and life and what they are doing with it. God's Word did that in New Testament times. It can do it again today.

God spoke to me

All this raises a fundamental issue: how can the modern Christian claim that Scripture can guide him in the details of his daily living? After all, this is what we are assuming in the whole process; that I may ask not just 'What did it say?' but also 'What is it saying?' Certainly the way in which we stress scriptural preaching and daily personal Bible reading implies that God can speak to me, personally, through this book. The question is, 'How does the Holy Spirit make God's will known to me through the Bible?'

A Christian mind

Of course, as we have already seen, a general study of the Bible will gradually influence the way in which we think and the way in which we approach life. The average Christian builds up his or her knowledge of the Bible over the years, coming upon one truth after another, having lessons reiterated and reinforced in all kinds of ways until he or she begins to 'think biblically'. If I am prepared to allow the truths of Scripture to judge the way in which I live, including those standards, outlooks and values which I have inherited from my own time, the Bible will begin to shape my daily behaviour. I will begin to obey the voice of God even though this means denying the many other voices which clamour for my attention. As Tony Thiselton puts it, 'Because the Bible makes him into a person of Christian mind, the Christian may reflect responsibly and rationally about God's will in and for the present.'[15]

When my girls were young, they would ask for all kinds of things which they would not dream of asking for today, simply because they had not learnt, through the trial and error of growing up, something of my 'mind'. In a similar way, Christian maturity brings with it a developing understanding of God's mind.

Divine underlining

Christians, however, have often claimed more than this. How often do we hear the Bible expounded and feel that a particular truth is especially relevant to our *current* situation? Many also testify that God can and does make his will known through the devotional reading of Scripture, and that we may receive guidance for the details of our lives in this way. 'The verse seemed to stand out' is the sort of thing we often say. Is this justifiable or just wishful thinking? Is it really the Holy Spirit speaking, or is it, as some have suggested, that the Scriptures merely become a psychological sounding-board for our own unconscious, making us more self-aware?

The Bible tells us that God rules in human affairs. What is more, he is not just concerned with events on a world scale. He looks after the details of ordinary Christian experience. For the individual Christian all things *do* work together to fulfil God's purpose in his or her life. If this is the case, we must expect it to apply particularly when that Christian turns for guidance to the book through which God comes to us and reveals himself to us – the Bible. There is a fundamental 'seek and you shall find' concept involved here.

God in my life

More than this, the indwelling of the believer by the Holy Spirit introduces an immediacy, a moment by moment pattern, into the Christian's experience which makes the daily details of his life significant. Coincidence becomes a commonplace phenomenon. Answered prayer becomes a reality. There is a divine dimension to life which puts him in

[15] In J. R. W. Stott (ed.), *Obeying Christ in a Changing World* (Collins, 1977), p.118.

touch with a reality which cannot be seen, but which nevertheless makes itself known at every turn. The passage for the day or the text of the sermon are parts of an intricate divinely woven web of which we perceive fragments here and there, and yet these fragments have the unmistakable mark of God's handiwork.

Sometimes the believer is confronted by God and his claims when he is not directly looking for them. On occasions God's Word surprises us with a new and delightful discovery which encourages us and reassures us. At other times it has all the force and conviction, not to say dread, of a confronting challenge. This is one of the reasons why the Christian can hear and read the Bible over and over again without tiring. The same passage may speak to us in different ways, because our personal circumstances change, and we are at a different stage along the Christian way.

Danger!

The very real danger in this approach is, of course, its subjectivity. To claim that 'God spoke to me' is to claim that God is authorizing my decisions and actions, and we know only too well that, as human beings, we can be easily mistaken. It is desperately easy to read into a text just what we want to find there. Sally was very friendly with a Christian family who had left their church in a huff. While staying at their house, she read a verse from Deuteronomy in her *Daily Light*, 'You shall never return that way again.' It seemed obvious to her that this was guidance for her to leave the church too. Quite apart from the horoscope approach to the Bible, she had simply applied this in the way she had wanted to. For instance, it never occurred to her that, if God was speaking through the verse, 'that way' could equally apply to the house in which she was staying!

It is interesting to see that Jesus himself was actually tempted to misuse Scripture in this way. It is a sobering reminder that 'the devil can cite Scripture for his purpose'.[16]

---

[16] Luke 4:911; *cf.* W. Shakespeare, *The Merchant of Venice*, 1.3.

Are there any safeguards against this kind of thing? Perhaps the most readily available check is that God is a God of truth, and because of this he does not contradict himself. If he is speaking to me through the Bible by the Holy Spirit, then what he says will be consistent with what he has already said. The more I know the mind of God from the Word of God, the less likely shall I be tempted to claim some personal revelation which reverses what he has already given.

This, incidentally, is what Pauline at the very beginning of our book should have remembered. Sex outside of marriage is quite clearly wrong according to the Bible. So, however sincere John may have been in thinking that God had told him otherwise, he was mistaken. *God does not contradict himself.*

In this respect, the young Christian can be in particular danger in that his understanding of Scripture is necessarily limited. We all testify to the kindness and long-suffering of a heavenly Father when we look back to the earliest years of our Christian lives. The remarkable thing is not that we made mistakes, but that we did not make more!

The Christian community

Another God-given check is the fact that we are not just isolated individuals when it comes to understanding the Bible. The Holy Spirit who indwells us also makes us members of Christ's church. As such we can hear God's Word explained week by week as well as being heirs to a wealth of Christian understanding which comes to us, from the past, in the form of books and commentaries. We belong to one another for our own good. In the living, loving fellowship of a group of believers the individual can be directed and corrected in his belief and in his behaviour.

Make up your own mind

Having said this, individual believers also have both the liberty and the duty to study the Bible for themselves, and not to swallow any particular doctrinal line wholesale. For example, the Reformers pioneered the idea of 'popular' translations so that anyone might be able to read the Bible, to 'test all things' that came their way. As we have noted, they believed – somewhat naïvely it seems to us now – that the Bible was plain enough for every sincere believer to draw the same conclusions and come to a common faith. After all, every believer was indwelt by the same Spirit.

Disagreements

Even in their own day this proved to be far too idealistic, although the vast majority of Protestants did seize the essential truths. Since that time, the wide variety of conclusions drawn by 'Bible-believing' Christians has made some people sceptical about the whole principle of 'private judgment', as it was called. Surely, runs the argument, if there is no check on interpretation, the result is the splintering of God's people into a multitude of groups, each believing their own thing. All this is sadly true. Protestants seem to have a genius for division in this way. It is equally true that the Roman Church, which claimed to have the same beliefs throughout, kept the inroads of modernism at bay for considerably longer, although in recent years we have seen even Catholic scholars questioning the authority of both Bible and pope.

We sometimes seem to forget that people always have had their differences. In New Testament days both truth and error were current. The early Christians were repeatedly warned against false teachers and unsound doctrine.[17] They were also required to think through their own beliefs. The Beroeans, who checked up on Paul's ministry by reading the Bible for themselves, are the prototype for private judgment, and they were commended for it.[18]

Authority

The alternative is to submit not only one's judgment but also one's conscience to someone else, whether it be church, preacher or pope. Many a group has gone off the rails when individual members have submitted themselves without question to powerful personality leadership, especially when

[17] For example, 2 Corinthians 11:13-15; Galatians 1:6-9; Philippians 3:18-19; 2 Thessalonians 2:1-3; 2 Timothy 3:1-9; 2 Peter 2:1-3; 1 John 2:18ff.; etc.   [18] Acts 17.11.

claims to immediate God-given revelation have been thrown in. The same thing happened in New Testament times and stress had to be placed on *personal* obedience to Christ and his word. They had to be reminded that whereas God gave the church overseers, their job was to direct the believers' attention away to Christ not to themselves. 'Ministers' are, by definition, not masters but servants; stewards in God's household who will one day answer for their stewardship.[19]

We cannot shelve the responsibility for thinking for ourselves by submitting ourselves to others who profess to do our thinking for us. We have one Lord; that is Christ, and one day we shall each give him an account of our actions. This is the sort of thing Martin Luther had in mind when he protested, 'My conscience has been taken captive by the Word of God and I neither can nor will recant, since it is neither safe nor right to act against conscience.'

Pat was a student nurse and enjoying it, until the elder in her fellowship had 'a word from the Lord' that she should give it up and stop working. Because she respected him and submitted to his authority, she not only ignored the clear command of Scripture to work for our living if we have the opportunity,[20] she ended up on the dole, living off others. Once again, God cannot be saying two things at once, and sometimes we need the courage of our convictions to say, 'God has already made the issue quite clear. Any other course of action is wrong.' Unfortunately, like the courtiers in Hans Christian Andersen's tale about the emperor's invisible clothes, we do not want to appear fools – or unspiritual – by pointing out the facts. Because of this, some of the most stupid things have been done in the name of Christ, and God's people have allowed them to happen unchallenged.

I admire the courage of a young friend of mine who was brought up to believe that there were no other Christians outside the Closed Brethren group in which she had been reared. She had trusted Christ and loved her Bible, and it became clear to her as time went by that she was being asked to do things which in her view were not scriptural. To leave

[19] 1 Corinthians 4:1-2.   [20] See 2 Thessalonians 3:6-13.

the church, however, meant leaving home and family as well as all she had known as fellowship. Yet she did it, and God honoured her faith by giving her in a thousand ways all that she had lost in the process.

They can't all be right!

Our problem is that we hear a variety of voices, often seeming reasonable, not to say spiritual, and yet just as often contradicting one another. Some maintain one particular emphasis. Some stress half-truths. Some reflect the intellectual fashions of the day, but many are exclusive in their claims upon our conscience, and all in some measure make Scripture their starting-point.

One thing is certain: they cannot all be right; but then, neither need they all be entirely wrong. It falls to the individual to decide for himself or herself. Even the 'soundest' teacher has his particular likes and dislikes.

Discernment

All this seems excessively individualistic, but there are certain safety factors. As we have said, most of us accumulate a varied spiritual education as we grow older. Books we read, preachers we hear, magazines we pick up, as well as our daily study of the Bible – often with the help of notes – all steer us in certain directions, and all ought to make us more discerning. We begin to recognize God's truth and to smell error when it comes our way. At the same time, whoever we are, we become aware that our insight is limited. This realization should lead us to a true sense of humility when we propound our views and also make us ready to learn from others.

The whole truth?

Then again, we can be fairly certain that no one particular line of interpretation is infallible, especially if it claims *exclusively* to have cornered the whole of God's truth. There seems to be a subtle psychology in some theological positions. Some people, by their very temperament, tend to polarize in their convictions and fall into opposite camps which are mutually exclusive. This ought to warn us against trying to shut all God's truth up in a particular box. As we have already said, no human scheme, no human system ever yet constructed, has been big enough to contain the many-sidedness of God's self-revelation.

At the level of Christian understanding, Paul's picture of the church as *a body* tells us that we have so much to give to one another. We need one another's points of view to round out our grasp of the truth. It would certainly be wrong to take and boast over a particular stance, dismissing another's convictions, without carefully thinking through all the arguments. The person who sees only his side of the issue has only half of the story. Church history is littered with examples of theological opponents who all had something valuable to say, but who would not listen to any other viewpoint but their own.

The most fruitful approach is carefully to choose the best from any and every tradition. We may recognize that, whereas no-one may have the whole truth, many have particular insights because of their different vantage-points. We know that, in the past, even those with heretical views were often only over-stressing one particular neglected aspect of truth. That is why heresy is sometimes so difficult to pin down. It begins with a truth which is perfectly true in itself. This is not to say that we may abandon those fundamental issues about which the Bible is reasonably clear, but it does mean that we should recognize that we are not the first or the only Christians, and that we have a rich heritage to possess and to use.

What we have inherited

It was this heritage which became a bone of contention at the time of the Reformation, largely because of differing estimates of its value. The Roman Catholic Church at that time, as today, looked upon the accumulated teaching of the Church (including its creeds and the statements of its councils) as being an extension of God's revelation through the living, speaking voice of the Church. (Nowadays this has come to include 'official' pronouncements by the pope.) In this view, Scripture itself is only *part* of what God has revealed to us.

The Reformers themselves did not despise these traditions. John Calvin, for example, had a very wide knowledge of medieval theology, and he was prepared to put it to use when working out his own. For them, however, Scripture was in a class of its own; and tradition, while sometimes being helpful in understanding Scripture, was secondary and fallible. This was reasonably obvious to them, since parts of that tradition actually contradicted the teaching of the Bible.

Double-think

Later on, Protestants became guilty of double-think. As far as these ancient teachings were concerned, they were often neglected. When it came to 'Protestant tradition', however, even though this could be fairly diverse in expression, the opposite line was taken, no doubt on the grounds that such tradition must be 'biblical'. We still live with remnants of that attitude today. Some evangelicals will fiercely adhere to a particular approach to biblical truth without realizing that it may be as much tradition as the teaching of the Fathers. One of the danger signs is when we refuse to face up to what Scripture says. If your system demands that you explain away or adjust aspects of what the Bible says, it is a sure indication that you are shaping Scripture to your tradition. Sometimes the traditional way in which we look at some passages actually obscures their meaning, and prevents us from grasping the original impact.

Tony Thiselton cites the example of the parable of the Pharisee and the publican.[21] Because of our traditional understanding of Pharisees as proud and hypocritical religious prigs, we expect Jesus to condemn the Pharisee. The crowds who heard Jesus would have expected *the very opposite*. For them a Pharisee was a model of upright, religious living. We find it difficult to recapture the shock and consternation that Jesus' words would have provoked simply because of our interpretative tradition.

A good illustration of this is the debate which is going on at present about spiritual gifts. Many of us have inherited a

[21] A. C. Thiselton in I. H. Marshall (ed.), *New Testament Interpretation*, pp.90ff.; Luke 18:9-14.

tradition which says that God gave the church gifts such as prophecy and tongues for use until we had a New Testament. Then he withdrew most of them because they were no longer necessary. On this showing, anyone who claims to have such gifts must be self-deceived or even of the devil. There is absolutely nothing in the New Testament itself, however, to support such a tradition. The verses usually quoted certainly do not mean this.[22] They have simply been used to explain the strange silence of history in this matter.

On the other hand, this does not mean that the only alternative is the equally traditional Pentecostal understanding of spiritual gifts. In this case the Scriptures are often used to underpin a doctrine derived from experience. Until we are ready to admit the weaknesses of *both* positions, we cannot really get back to what the Bible teaches on this subject.

The benefits
Tradition itself may not be a bad thing. The work that many have done before us can be of immense value when we come to understand the Bible for ourselves. Confessions, creeds, theological works and commentaries are all tools for us to use. The insights of other generations can sometimes be a healthy corrective to our own, but we must be prepared to test them all by the Word of God. If we do this we shall endorse some of them and discard others. We may find that we have to do the same with our particular traditions which we have unquestioningly inherited and adopted.

Using the tools
In practical terms, how can we begin to use this vast heritage of ours? What sort of equipment do we have at our disposal?

Versions
Beginning with the text of Scripture, it is a good thing to have more than one translation, and to compare them with one another. The Revised Standard Version or the New International Version brings us fairly near the original. Add to these the Good News Bible or a paraphrase such as

[22] 1 Corinthians 13:8-10; Hebrews 2:3-4.

J. B. Phillips' work, and you should get a reasonable idea of what the Bible says.

Language study

'Should I learn Greek and Hebrew?' is a question that I am often asked. There are some who feel that knowing the original language is a golden key to the mysteries of the Bible, and that is true up to a point. The ordinary Christian, however, is often so busy that he has no time to learn the language properly, or to keep it up afterwards. A working knowledge of the Bible languages is a lifetime's job. Get someone else to do it for you. (A minister, however, would find it very useful to come to grips with Greek, at least, if only to help him to use some of the more advanced commentaries. Get into the habit of doing a bit each day, and you will soon surprise yourself on how much you know.)

Background

Books on Bible background[23] help you to set the scene, as does a good Bible atlas, especially an illustrated one. Photographs of Bible locations enable you to get an idea of distances and size, and if you ever get the chance of going there yourself, take it with both hands.

Reference

Bible dictionaries often contain a wealth of information, not just the meaning of words, but also historical and cultural background which is invaluable.[24] A concordance will help you to look up a word wherever it comes in Scripture. It is useful to get one which refers to the Greek and Hebrew terms as well, as they are often translated by more than one English word. This is referred to as an 'analytical concordance'.[25]

Commentaries

When it comes to commentaries, once again we have an abundance in English. Some of the older ones are extremely

[23] For example: *The Lion Handbook to the Bible* (Lion Publishing, 1973). [24] See *The Illustrated Bible Dictionary* (3 vols., IVP, 1980). [25] *E.g.* R. Young, *Analytical Concordance to the Holy Bible* (Lutterworth, 1939).

valuable in that they seemed to be more concerned in those days about applying what the Bible says to life. There are also some recent works which do this well,[26] although the modern tendency has been to produce books which tell us what the Bible says rather than what it has to do with our present needs. Some of the one-volume commentaries are helpful, although you have to remember that if you are going to ask for the whole Bible to be covered in one book, you will not get much on each verse! It is better slowly to build up a collection of commentaries on individual books as you study them in turn.[27] Remember, too, that no-one has the last word. It is useful to compare commentary with commentary, especially in difficult areas.

Teaching books

On top of all these we have books on Bible teaching in general as well as studies on particular topics such as the Holy Spirit or the church in Scripture.[28] After all, you can either work steadily through a Bible book, or you can try and collect together all that Scripture has to say on one subject. Whichever way you do it, it is a good thing to keep notes. There are some guided studies which help you in this way.[29]

Travelling around the world, I have often realized just how well off we are as English-speakers. We have far more help in these ways than any other language group. It is the result of years of exacting study on the part of gifted men and women who have given their lives to the job. You may never be able to hear most of them preach or teach. Some have already died. But you can still benefit from their ministry. If we must really answer for all the spiritual opportunities which come our way, we shall be more guilty than most if we neglect them. On the other hand, it gives us the immense privilege as well as the responsibility of being able to dig out the truth for ourselves, not just for our own sakes, but that we might in turn share it with others.

[26] *E.g. The Bible Speaks Today* series (IVP). [27] See especially the *Tyndale* series of Bible commentaries; the *New International* series of commentaries (Eerdmans). [28] *E.g.* G. E. Ladd, *A Theology of the New Testament* (Eerdmans, 1974); the *Kingsway Bible Teaching* series. [29] *E.g.* A. M. Stibbs (ed.), *Search the Scriptures* (IVP, 1967); P. Lee, G. Scharf and R. Willcox, *Food for Life* (IVP, 1977).

5

Answering today's problems

In the Third World, particularly in Latin America, we are seeing a reaction away from traditional interpretation with such movements as the self-styled 'theology of liberation'. Instead of beginning with the Bible and going to the world, these theologians claim to reverse the process. They start with the questions the world is asking, and then go to the Bible for the answers. Living as many of them do in unjust and corrupt societies which have been propped up for years by the church, they have reason to believe that the traditional approach has never come to terms with the real problem.

This highlights our last topic. How do we apply Bible teaching to the sort of situation we find in our modern world, especially when the Bible does not give us any direct advice on a particular matter?

Straight teaching
First of all, let us point out that there are no short cuts. In no way can we dispense with the hard, methodical work of straightforward exegesis, asking what the Bible says. If we did this more thoroughly and consistently, we should probably have fewer problems. As we have said, when we begin to think biblically we start to see the whole situation from God's point of view.

Again, as Jews and Christians have recognized for years, there are a whole number of issues where the Bible teaching is quite clear cut. We can apply it directly to the situation we find ourselves in today.

Take a simple topic like murder. There can be no argument that the Bible teaches that we must not take the life of another. 'You shall not kill' is fairly straightforward for most of us![1] Of course, you need to put a verse like this in the wider context of the Old Testament. From the other regulations we find there, this excluded both capital punishment and war. Some would say that even these are included by Jesus' teaching on this verse, although he was more concerned with underlying motives and attitudes.[2] So, if I am tempted to murder my wife or my next-door neighbour, I know that it would be clearly wrong in God's sight.

If you want a modern extension, surely abortion comes in here. I had a young lady justifying abortion on demand to me recently, protesting that 'every child should be a wanted child'. I agreed, but I went on to point out that this does not mean that we can kill off the ones we do not want. In Scripture God alone is entitled to take life, not man.

We might include here *inferred teaching* on particular issues. Take this business of whom a Christian should marry. We are quite clearly warned against getting closely involved with unbelievers.[3] We know that a Christian widow could remarry only if the man was a Christian.[4] And we see some of the problems that arise when only one partner becomes a Christian.[5] The whole thing adds up to Christians marrying Christians.

Thinking it through
Sometimes we have to deal with a situation which they simply did not have in biblical times.[6] Take the issue of trade unionism, which is a fact of life in western society, and a real issue in the lives of many working (and sometimes striking) Christians. The economic system in the New Testament was based on a pattern of slavery which has fortunately passed from the scene. The advice that Peter and Paul gave to Christian slaves cannot be transferred directly to another system.

What we have to do is to go behind the particulars of Bible teaching to those general principles which apply universally. In this case, we should need to see what the Bible has to say

[1] Exodus 20:13. [2] Matthew 5:21-22. [3] 2 Corinthians 6:14-16. [4] 1 Corinthians 7:39. [5] 1 Corinthians 7:12-16. [6] See studies such as D. Field, *Free to do right* (IVP, 1973); G. W. Kirby, *Understanding Christian Ethics* (SU, 1973); F. Colquhoun (ed.), *Moral Questions* (Falcon, 1976).

about work, both in the Old Testament and in the New. We should need to think through what is involved when God expects us to be righteous, whether we are employers or employees. This will mean that, as individuals, we have certain rights and, what is often forgotten, certain responsibilities too. It has a great deal of bearing on, for example, keeping or breaking contracts, or what is a fair wage for the job.

The Bible also teaches about the temptation to be greedy. It has things to say about loyalty and not letting other people down. It equally tells us that we do not live or act alone, that we have a solidarity with other people, and that we are responsible to and for one another. Most of all, it tells us of the possibility of Christian loving overcoming natural barriers, and even coping with people who hate and oppose us.

Principles, not rules

All these principles come together and modify one another. Let us remember that principles are not rules. They are considerations which have to be borne in mind when looking for an answer. If I am a loving employer, I shall be concerned about the best interests of my employees. But it would be irresponsible if, out of love, I paid them more than the firm was earning. I equally have a responsibility to keep the ship afloat, or everyone might lose their jobs.

Sometimes, in the imperfect world in which we live, we have to opt for the least of the evils rather than what is the absolute best. It is here that biblical principles can help us to come to a decision. Christian doctors are continually having to struggle with this one. With all that I have already said about abortion, for example, there are times when things are not quite so straightforward. If it is a case of saving the life of either the child, or the mother who has other children and family responsibilities, they would opt for the latter – sadly, but with a clear conscience that they did the best thing in the circumstances.

Putting it together

There are occasions when the problems demand that we consider both straight biblical teaching and biblical principles. Take the case of homosexuality. We can begin with the general principle that when God designed the human race, he intended it to be heterosexual.[7] More than this, it is assumed all through the Bible that men and women will find natural expression for their sexuality in marriage and a family. If this is the case (except for that tiny minority of human beings who are born with indeterminate sex, which is something rather different), homosexuality must be unnatural and unnecessary. This is borne out, of course, by the fact that there are some societies where it is unknown.

More than this, we have some very explicit, straight forward teaching about the homosexual *act*. In the Old Testament it was a capital offence,[8] while in the New, Paul lists it among those things which will take us to hell,[9] linking it with the godless excesses of idolatry.[10] More positively, however, he also tells us that the power of Christ can deliver people from this perversion[11] – and a good number of others – and by the Holy Spirit remake them in the image of God.

Perhaps it is at this last stage that we come up most against the spirit of the age by which we have all been conditioned. We have been told from childhood that we are the product of the genes we inherit and the atmosphere in which we were brought up, and nothing can change that. The New Testament message challenges that kind of psychological determinism. By the grace of God we *can* change. That is what the Bible is all about.

For we have to come back to some very basic questions when we study the Bible – such as 'Did God really mean what he said?', 'Are his promises true?' 'Are his warnings still valid?' If we take the Bible seriously, we can answer these questions in only one way, and that is by obedient faith, taking God at his word, expecting him to act, and above all, *doing what he says*!

One of the strengths of the Latin American movement we have mentioned above is that they insist that the theologian cannot stand aloof from the needs of his own time, and that is equally true of the ordinary Christian. We must work out the

[7] Genesis 1:26-27.   [8] Leviticus 18:22; 20:13.   [9] 1 Corinthians 6:9-10.   [10] Romans 1:26-27.   [11] 1 Corinthians 6:11.

94

implications of what we learn from God's Word, in spite of the fact that it might cost us a great deal to do so. In that respect they have caught something of the spirit of Jesus and the prophets who 'died before their time because of their theologizing'.[12] What they had to say about God and his demands cut so close that their own contemporaries could not take it. Whatever the cost, what we learn from the Bible we must relate to life.

Summing it all up

As we come to the end of this book, some might feel that, although they are Christians, they are completely incompetent when it comes to the matter of interpreting the Bible for themselves. With all this talk about languages and world-views and the rest, surely the whole business is now the province of the scholar. What hope has even the intelligent lay person of understanding God's Word on his or her own? In the old days it seemed so simple. You just prayed for light and read the book. But now it appears to be so complicated.

Once again we need to get this thing into perspective. The Reformers were surely right when they believed that Scripture was written plainly enough to give the simplest, sincere believer what he needed to be saved. We have many a testimony from people who had little or no religious background, and who were converted to Christ through reading the Bible alone. On top of that, there is quite enough to get us going on the Christian way. But the honest inquirer will sooner or later come up against passages which are hard to understand. At that point he has the choice between ignoring them, working out some scheme of his own, or using the tools available in order to come to a better understanding.

Too many Christians take the first option, which is really a refusal to think through their faith. A good number have taken the second and have wandered into By-path Meadow as a result. Whereas the third does not promise to give us all the answers, it may at least save us from one-sided errors, and give us a far bigger view of God's truth than we could

[12] J. L. Segundo, *The Liberation of Theology* (Gill and Macmillan, 1977), p.26.

have come to unaided.

In that way, biblical studies, especially as they come to us in the form of translations, commentaries and helps, are an extension of the ministry of the church. For we are not alone in this. We belong to one another, sharing a common heritage and a common destiny. We belong to the church of Jesus Christ, and the Lord of that church has given to some gifts for its upbuilding and maturing.[13] Not everybody is a Bible scholar any more than everybody is a minister, but everybody should be able to benefit from their work.

Equally the scholar needs the ordinary Christian. Too many who are involved in biblical research are one stage removed from real life. We can be deceived into thinking that we are ministering to Christ's body when we are really only talking to one another! If the need of the ordinary Christian is instruction and teaching, the need of the scholar is relevance and application. The place where we can meet, of course, is within the fellowship of God's people. There we can minister to one another, and there we can work together for the extension of Christ's kingdom here on earth.

[13] Ephesians 4:1-11ff.